ED SMITH is a renowned t
played cricket for Kent, Mid
Selector for England cricke
unprecedented success for En
director of the Institute of Sp
five books, including *What Sport Tells Us About Life* (Penguin, 2008), and is a contributing writer for the *New Statesman*.

Praise for *Making Decisions*:

'A masterful combination of analysis and personal experience of decision-making at the highest level. Full of insights, wisdom and highly entertaining' MERVYN KING

'An absolutely fascinating book' The Game, *The Times* podcast

'Sincere and often self-reflective … offers genuine searing insight, making points you feel have never been made before. A learned and engaging study of decision-making'
New Statesman

'An excellent read … based on his years as England's chief cricket selector, but drawing on much broader thinking on decision-making' SIMON KUPER

'In this fascinating and highly readable book, Ed Smith explores how the human and the machine can work together'
MATT RIDLEY

'A terrific, enriching book' PETER OBORNE

Making Decisions

Thinking Bigger
Seeing Further

Ed Smith

William Collins
An imprint of HarperCollins*Publishers*
1 London Bridge Street
London SE1 9GF

WilliamCollinsBooks.com

HarperCollins*Publishers*
Macken House, 39/40 Mayor Street Upper
Dublin 1, D01 C9W8, Ireland

First published in Great Britain in 2022 by William Collins
This William Collins paperback edition published in 2023

1

A catalogue record for this book is
available from the British Library

ISBN 978-0-00-853018-1

Set in Adobe Calson Pro
Printed and bound in the UK using 100%
renewable electricity at CPI Group (UK) Ltd

This book is produced from independently certified FSC™ paper
to ensure responsible forest management.

For more information visit: www.harpercollins.co.uk/green

For the students, teachers and staff at the
Institute of Sports Humanities

Having lots of ideas doesn't mean you're clever, any more than having lots of soldiers means you're a good general.

Nicolas Chamfort, *Maximes et Pensées*

Contents

1
Where Do 'We' Fit In?

If my heart could do the thinking
And my head begin to feel

Van Morrison

'How much longer until the selection of cricket teams is done entirely by an algorithm?'

That question was put to me in early 2020 by an Australian investor, in his house overlooking the Melbourne Cricket Ground where I'd spent the day watching an England cricket team – selected by humans, I should add – play against its Australian counterpart.

The table went quiet. A cricket selector, like an active investor, is paid to deliver superior judgements that improve overall performance. But can't these decisions now be outsourced to a self-learning machine? After all, capturing data of all kinds is getting easier and cheaper in every industry, allowing Artificial Intelligence (AI) to expand and improve. So in the age of big data and machine learning, what role – if any – will there be for human intelligence?

Quite simply, where do 'we' fit in?

In board games, the balance of power between human and machine intelligence shifted irrevocably in 1997 when IBM's computer Deep Blue beat chess grandmaster Garry Kasparov. In his last game against Deep Blue, Kasparov lasted a mere 19 moves, conceding that he'd 'lost his fighting spirit'. Other complex board games followed. In 2016, the world's top Go player was defeated by AlphaGo – a program developed by the AI start-up DeepMind (acquired by Google for $600 million in 2014). Is aptitude at games a metaphor for the fate of human intelligence, struggling on for a while against machine learning, before eventually suffocating like a canary in the coal mine?

Is this really the future we face as humans? After all, one computer versus one human is only part of the story. Life is infinitely more complex. In most decision-making contexts we arrange ourselves in groups and teams, and can blend differing types of intelligence or skills as we see fit. What's the best formula overall? Kasparov's response to losing to Deep Blue was to invent 'advanced chess', in which both human players arm themselves with a computer, therefore engaging against their rival human-computer team. The experience taught Kasparov that the real value of the human, in this set-up, is creativity; he had a computer for all the rest.

It's now established that in chess a hybrid team, with people to command strategy and computers to execute tactics, is superior to either a grandmaster or a computer on its own.

How much is cricket like chess, and how much are games a good analogy for the rest of life? There are always differences. Unlike cricket, chess is a completely 'bounded' game, with perfect information and no variance in conditions or vulnerability to luck. Unexpected rain, or an unpredictable easterly wind, can't suddenly change the dimensions of the board, or swing the match towards white.

But despite the differences between the games, Kasparov's point about creativity is close to what I've observed in a sport too often beset by the phrase 'rain stopped play'. I've arrived at the view that the 'edge' in high-performance sport lies in the interaction of different kinds of intelligence. As always, that includes distinct kinds of human intelligence, but now with the added extra question of how people and machines can come together effectively – algorithms *in tandem* with intuition, not algorithms *instead* of intuition.

This has implications for the types of people we will need at the heart of decision-making. Can you bring the human perspective – creativity, imagination and the ability to sense intuitively if something is *loosely* right or wrong? But can you also follow highly technical and data-rich information, and communicate meaningfully with experts who are trained to be impatient with approximate knowledge? This kind of thinker, acting as a bridge and reconciler of differing kinds of intelligence, has the best shot at the decision-making sweet spot.

'Faster horse'?

In spring 2018, I was appointed as National Selector for England cricket, with responsibility for picking squads for the England men's teams. It was widely reported, even before we'd selected our first squad, that selection was now going to become dominated by data. Perhaps the fact that I'd written a book about baseball, the foundational sport when it comes to data analytics, was a contributing factor to this belief. And as captain of Middlesex in 2008, taking a contrarian approach to T20 cricket selection (drawing on data from the Indian Premier League), we'd won the domestic T20 tournament.

Now, apparently, the new selection panel were going to use a highly analytical approach to choosing England cricketers. The system was 'long overdue modernisation' or risked ruin from 'left-field scientific methods' that were 'too clever by half'. The debate was ready to spark, and all we had to do was light the match.

The relationship between what we decide – the positions we take, the moves we make – and life as it unfolds has always been a central preoccupation, perhaps *the* central human preoccupation. A version of this question, of course, has always been with us. But the debate about the scope of human agency is entering a wholly new phase, and where 'we fit in here' is becoming less and less clear. With the emergence of machine learning, the human mind's ability to direct the world around us – and to make sense of events by doing so – is being reshaped in revolutionary and disorientating ways. In commercial activity, the real battleground is increasingly to own and monetise the imprint left by people's internet history. Our value, at least as potential customers, is unearthed in the footprint of our virtual steps. As a result of this data gold rush, skill and insight are increasingly seen as inferior to simple possession … the possession of *data*.

This has profound consequences for identity as well as decisions. Decision-making has always been innately connected to the way we understand and make sense of our experience. The perception of 'agency' is central to how we perceive ourselves. In retelling the story of our lives inside our heads, we are constantly revisiting and revising how decisions played out, how we could have done things differently or better.

But what if human intelligence is perceived as being increasingly marginalised, even irrelevant? That's why the spectre of machine learning implicitly threatens our collective self-confidence. Are we entering an era of gradually diminishing human self-determinism, a depressing reverse-Renaissance, with the machine cast as our new god and master? In this context, the trajectory, relevance and even survival of human judgement is a debate that applies to every area of modern life.

Games have always been a laboratory for the study of decision-making. Girolamo Cardano, a sixteenth-century gambler, wrote the first great book on chance and the odds. If humans could get better at understanding probability, it opened up thrilling new possibilities. Today, paradoxically, if a computer can teach itself to master probability, then human potential is pushed right on to the back foot: the issue becomes 'What's left for us to do?'

In reply to the question posed at the very beginning – when will humans be replaced by an algorithm? – I said that England cricket, at that moment, did gain a performance 'edge' from the pragmatic use of data, and, yes, as we'll see later in this book, this did sometimes involve input from algorithms. The selectors benefited from data in a variety of different contexts, including expanding the scope of our thinking: computers, unlike humans, look at everything (and without preconceptions). And there is, undeniably, still opportunity to get even more value out of data within cricket decision-making.

But I do not believe that information derived from an algorithm will enhance performance *unless* it is intelligently assessed and critically scrutinised by human beings. Data is useful – but only if you know how to harness it. Judgement – the framing of the appropriate question as well as the pursuit of the best available answer – is always to the fore. Humans aren't finished yet.

Further, not only does the human dimension remain central and intrinsic to good decisions: decision-making is also increasingly bound up with being human. *The more we understand what machines can do, the more it shines a light on the special qualities of human intelligence: imagination, analogy, making unpredictable connections.* That's the flip side of understanding data: it encourages us to stay close to those things that only humans can do. Understanding this paradox, central to *Making Decisions*, requires a strange mixture of humility and boldness.

When I started out as a selector in cricket, and making decisions became the focus of my professional life, I didn't anticipate coming to see decision-making through the lens of creativity. But now I do. As a result, *Making Decisions* is as much about the creative process as it is about systems and techniques.

The question of creativity within cricket selection unexpectedly reconnected me with my roots. My father is a novelist, my mother an art teacher. Over time, I learnt to listen to those strands of my character, too. An effective decision-maker needs an authentic voice, a style and approach that is unique to them – just like an athlete or an artist. Instead of paraphrasing an algorithm, we have to add value to it.

When the England and Wales Cricket Board (ECB) entered a new partnership with Microsoft in 2020, I was asked to give a presentation to the new high-performance task force comprising ECB data analysts and Microsoft AI engineers. The mission was to build a self-teaching computer program that would be able to inform decision-making for England's cricket teams. So I began by quoting Henry Ford's classic saying about the invention of the mass-produced motor car: 'If I'd asked people what they wanted, they'd have said a faster horse.'

'Hang on a minute,' I added. 'As a cricket selector who's now looking at building an algorithm for cricket decision-making, there's a potential irony here: am I like the horse in Ford's story? If this project completely succeeds, will we no longer need selectors to make cricketing judgements any more because AI will be doing it better?'

But that moment is not only a very long way off, I doubt it will ever arrive. Instead, using sport as a testing ground, *Making Decisions* argues that the best decisions flow from the skilful blend of differing kinds of intelligence – from algorithms to creative intuition. The ability to weigh and reconcile the artistic and scientific strands of decision-making is itself a distinct art – and close to the heart of the matter. 'You have to work out what humans are good at and what the model is good at,' argued Daryl Morey, the sports data pioneer who transformed basketball.

No one can tell you exactly how to make those assessments about who – or what – to listen to and when. Every context is different and unique. But you can, with the right frameworks, think better about how you are going to approach decisions. And the approach – the term 'process' is very incomplete, though obviously process is part of it – constitutes a significant proportion of what's under our control. It is similar to a batter hitting a cricket ball. The final connection, whether the shot is pure and clean, depends on readiness, movement and trust long before the strike of bat on ball. A decision-maker, too, seeks to arrive in sync and rhythm with the demands of the moment – well positioned, well armed and combining narrow focus with wider awareness.

My time as England selector was a fascinating moment to be a decision-maker in sport, at the cusp of an increasingly data-rich world. On the one hand, there was inevitable contrast with the past: how did the kinds of decisions we were making diverge from the decisions previously made by other selectors? On the other hand, how did current decisions – shaped by enduring belief in the value of human judgement – diverge from the positions that machine learning might arrive at in the future?

Our overall approach rested on the coexistence of two different forms of independence. In being prepared to arrive at judgements perceived as 'left-field', we embraced independence from conventional preconceptions about both players and team formation. And we didn't go along with the rationalist belief – or hope, in some quarters – that humans were increasingly irrelevant, and that 'judgements' are no better than 'biases' with convenient narratives attached. I have never believed that decision-making in cricket should – or could – be recast as a discipline within the natural sciences. Cricket contains threads that are inherently unpredictable, messy and uncertain – human to the core.

The combination of these two positions – first, that some judgements are intrinsically superior to others; second, that there is no perfect (or even knowable) 'system' – disappoints both extremes in the cartoonish 'data versus common sense' argument. You are, in effect, owning two forms of risk simultaneously: the final decision being taken and the (sometimes intuitive) method that led to it. Though often lonely, this is the pragmatic place to be.

This leads to a paradox within *Making Decisions*. To continue to add value, a decision-maker must remain open to insights and surprise connections – exactly the patterns of thought which can be hard to describe, let alone quantify. So in one sense I am setting myself a difficult challenge in writing about them. Where an algorithm can be completely described and explained, the imaginative dimension cannot. But that is bound up with its usefulness. 'Anything that we know how we do, machines will do better,' Kasparov argued in 2019. 'Now, the key element of this phrase is, "We know how we do ..." Because we do many things without knowing exactly how we do them.' Put differently, it is being *more* human, not less, that provides protection against becoming irrelevant.

An intriguing pattern within England's new selection approach from 2018 *was that there was no obvious pattern*. In the first year, we selected three new players aged 20 or younger to make Test debuts, which had never happened in history. But we also brought experienced players back from the wilderness – including one who had last played for England nine years previously (the second-longest gap of any international player from any nation).

Yet while the individual profiles of these players varied enormously, the guiding principle was always the same. What did the England team need, now and in the future? The 'right' player to select would only emerge after we'd first grappled hard with the team dimension. Instead of beginning with an abstract wish list ('We want players who are like this ...'), our starting point was 'What does the team need?' And the ability to stand back and see the wider picture – especially the complexity of team dynamics – remains very much the specialism of human beings, not algorithms.

History first, then strategy

My first decision was one that surprised some people: coming back to the sharp end of sport in the first place.

In early 2018, work was more varied and enjoyable than at any point in my life. I was writing a history book and columns for the *New Statesman* and the *Sunday Times*, I was about to launch an academic institute, and BBC Radio 4 had just commissioned me to present a new series called *The Ideas Lab*. And being a consultant in the Indian Premier League provided the adrenalin injection of high-performance sport. Working life was full, balanced and – even though I try to live with an open mind about the future – pretty much what I'd hoped for.

That was how things were when I got an email from Andrew Strauss, then Managing Director of the ECB, about the role of National Selector for England cricket. Strauss, alongside scouting guru Mo Bobat, was trying to create a modern system of selection that would improve England's performance across the board. They wanted to initiate something very different from what had come before, but still in tune with the innate characteristics of cricket as a game – a system with original aspects, but not new for the sake of it.

For starters, the new structure for selection would be entirely independent. Under the previous system, only one of the four selectors was dedicated full-time to England selection, with the second being the England head coach, and the third and fourth selectors simultaneously working as Directors of Cricket at county teams (the level below England teams). So one selector's primary expertise was coaching and two others were part-time.

Instead, the ECB now wanted to make selection a dedicated branch of high performance, constantly searching for an edge that would serve England's needs. Not only was the National Selector role expanded, but there would be a second full-time England selector (the role that James Taylor was later recruited to do and excelled at). This philosophical shift was in line with wider trends across sport. Football, baseball and basketball have all increasingly tilted their resources towards Player Identification (Player ID), recruitment and selection.

Initially, I said the new selector role wasn't for me because I was happily busy with other projects. And that was what I thought. But sometimes your heart takes control, and you feel more clearly than you can think. After that initial enquiry, I kept reflecting on England cricket and selection, how it could be done differently, and how the teams might evolve and win more. There was an urgency and attention whenever my thoughts turned to England, as though I was leaning forward inside my own head.

This book begins as it will continue, exploring differing kinds of decisions and how they can be approached. The foundational decision – whether to do the job in the first place – wasn't a question of weighing evidence, pros and cons, or detached analysis. I felt drawn in, engaged and absorbed. I was suddenly thinking about England cricket a great deal; nearly all the time. And I hadn't even put myself forward, let alone started. That's when you know that there isn't a decision to make after all. You've already made it. By the time I started the job officially, I'd already – in terms of thinking – been doing it for weeks.

Much of that thinking was about England's performances in recent years. Effective decision-making is usually bound up with an essential grasp of history. Successful selectors and coaches might hate 'history' as a subject, but they know they can't ignore history as a body of evidence. They are usually able to see patterns (often problematic patterns) in past performance and turn them into a kind of manifesto for the future.

That's also why arguments about the past form such an emotive and significant part of team life. In order to shape the future of the team, you'll almost certainly have to form a coherent picture of the team's past – and then persuade others that your interpretation of history is apt and true. Here history encounters psychology, and the process is rarely easy: most players (and employees more widely) construct their own versions of history to suit their own narratives and capabilities. The best strategists in sport are shrewd historians of *team success* and *team failure*.

History is vital to that other magic ingredient – vision. It is a cliché to want leaders with 'vision'. But vision is extremely difficult without a perceptive reading of the past; only then can good thinking be harnessed into a compelling vision of the future. Vision always follows from insight. The great sports coaches and strategists – before they address how to play in the upcoming matches – first find hidden truths in what has already happened.

This has nothing at all to do with book-learning or academia. (One of the difficulties with being considered 'academic' is the assumption that you rate academic knowledge more highly than experience and practical wisdom. I don't.) The central arguments about history in sport don't take place in books but inside the team and its management. When leaders begin to misinterpret the past, the team is likely to lose direction – and quickly. The same applies to business, and to any group of people loosely associated into a team of any kind.

A complexity here is that England cricket doesn't have one first team (like football), it has three: the Test team (five-day matches), the One Day International (ODI) team and the T20 team (the shortest format, 20 overs per side). We would have to understand each team on its own terms, while also working out how an overarching strategy could fit together collectively.

In spring 2018, those three England teams were at very different stages. The ODI side, flying high, was one year away from the definitive challenge of a World Cup. The T20 team, though feared and talented, hadn't yet become the powerhouse I believed it could be. The Test team had been struggling. Understanding each team's separate and distinct needs, as we will see, was central to the task. England selection, in the modern era of three formats, is significantly about nurturing players and maintaining high performance across all three codes simultaneously.

The Test team was going through one of its perennial existential crises. The Ashes series against Australia had just been lost 4–0 in the 2017–18 winter. Overall, in the three years before spring 2018, England had played 42 Tests, losing 20, winning 16 and drawing six. In terms of win–loss percentage over three years, the only teams in the world worse than England were Bangladesh, West Indies and Zimbabwe. In terms of matches won, every major Test nation was outperforming England.

Of England's 16 Test wins over three years, only three came overseas. In total, England had played 21 Tests abroad: three wins, 13 defeats, five draws. Home form remained consistently good. But the margin of defeat abroad, all taken together, was significantly greater than the margin of victory at home.

England's gradual Test decline certainly hadn't been caused by flashy or eye-catching strategy. England's selections, though it is always possible to argue about individual decisions, had mostly been fairly conventional and uncontroversial. Throughout those three years, England had mostly adopted the same players and similar team formations, whether the match was in Adelaide or London.

Why, I wondered, was there such reluctance, even when we were losing, to adopt alternative approaches for home and away conditions? With just three wins abroad and 13 defeats, was that approach still tenable?

Second, even clearer after the winter of 2017–18, England's Test bowling attack lacked variety. There was no express pace. The genuinely fast bowler Mark Wood was available, but he wasn't being selected. None of England's bowlers were left-handed, so opposition batters, once they had played themselves in, faced more and more of the same type of right-arm bowler, which was unlikely to upset the batters' rhythm. And there was no wrist-spinner (the ultimate game-changing skill). Adil Rashid, a wrist-spinner with the priceless ability to get anyone out at any time, had drifted out of the Test squad, despite being the top wicket-taker in the 2016–17 winter (with 38 wickets). Taken as a whole – although an individual case could be made for all the selected players – the Test team added up to *less* than the sum of its parts.

Third, England's Test team seemed to have an over-supply of good players in a few positions, and an under-supply of good players for other positions. That certainly wasn't the fault of the previous selectors, but I felt it could *inform* selection more.

Remarkably, a number of the leading middle-order batters in the country (Jonny Bairstow, Jos Buttler, Sam Billings, Ben Foakes and others) were also wicketkeepers. England's view in spring 2018 had been to pick just one of these talented players for the Test team and leave the others out in the cold.

But in other departments, the cupboard looked bare, especially at the top of the batting order. From 2012 to 2018, England selected and discarded a dozen top-order batters in the search for the long-term solutions as opening batters or at number three.

England's attitude to this unusual talent distribution seemed to be carry on as though things were normal, even though they weren't. Despite picking and dropping 12 players to bat in positions one, two and three, England seemed reluctant to abandon a policy of 'executive search'. We need people to bat in positions one, two and three – let's go and find them! But they couldn't be found.

There was, of course, an alternative logic available: instead of hoping they could invent a set of world-class top-order batters who didn't exist, England should focus on *deploying talent differently* rather than pretending they could simply *conjure up new talent*. Strategy should be informed by what's possible, not what you wish for.

This, then, was the underlying reality:

Players who don't exist can't be selected.

Home wins could no longer mask poor results abroad.

The XI should add up to more, not less, than the sum of its parts.

Selection had to be understood as a real-world puzzle rather than a fantasy executive search.

The team's needs should come first.

That, loosely, was my assessment of the England Test team in spring 2018. It hasn't changed much.

The ODI team, which was in irrepressible form, could not have been at a more different stage. It was approaching the high-jump bar and about to leap for glory. For the past three years, England's ODI team had been building both steadily and joyfully towards the World Cup – to be played on home soil in the UK in 2019.

The change of philosophy and performance of England's ODI team had been one of the most radical turnarounds in English cricket history. In previous cycles, England had clung to cautious and out-of-date tactics as the rest of the world had moved on without them. In the last three World Cups, England had entered every one with a low world ranking and performed correspondingly badly in the tournament itself.

Following the last debacle, at the 2015 World Cup, the ODI side had been completely reimagined. England now played a daring and risk-taking brand of ODI cricket, with batting talent right down the team list and a varied bowling attack. Crucially, Andrew Strauss as MD – alongside head coach Trevor Bayliss and captain Eoin Morgan – had significantly won the argument in terms of historical interpretation of past failings. Their aligned faith in a new style of play galvanised a sense of direction. Now, at this relatively late stage in that journey, just 14 months from the 2019 World Cup, England were on the brink of becoming the top-ranked ODI team in the world.

But the ODI side, though brimming with confidence and spectacular to watch, wasn't quite the complete article. If there was one area of weakness, it was fast bowling at the very beginning and the very end of the innings: a feared strike bowler who could stamp authority at the outset of the contest, and then return to the fray and finish the job when the game needed to be wrapped up.

The voice and character of the ODI side was fully formed and heading in exactly the right direction. But there was still scope to add star quality to the playing group – if, of course, any new player was good enough on merit to force their way into a team that was already breaking records and thrilling crowds.

England's T20 side, in my eyes, was a slightly curious case. Perhaps this was just a question of the rhythm of the international calendar. We were three years away from a T20 World Cup (due to be played in 2021), so the ODI World Cup of 2019 was the more pressing immediate priority. In recent months, perfectly understandably, important multi-format players had been rested for some T20 matches. But even allowing for the context of the World Cup cycles and the need to rest top talent occasionally, England's T20 team had even more power under the bonnet, waiting to be realised.

England were world-ranked fifth in T20s and I couldn't help asking myself the following question, looking at the devastating batting talent available to England: if a 50-over ODI match was shortened due to bad weather to a 20-over match (that is, a T20 in all but name), wouldn't England's chances of winning the match *increase* in the now abbreviated form? In other words, given England's playing talent, I felt that England could – perhaps should – be at least as good at T20s (world ranking five) as they were at ODIs (about to reach number one).

Further, could the T20 team double down on the same general approach (innovative and aggressive) that had taken the ODI side to the top of the world, only this time tweak the specifics to the unique and fast-changing challenges of T20?

Achieving this radicalisation of the existing template, however, might well demand making some tough calls on big-name players, and shuffling the pack towards an ultra-aggressive line-up (any change to the batting order creates losers as well as winners). So implementing such changes wasn't going to be easy, especially as the ODI side naturally remained the more urgent priority in the year leading up to the 2019 World Cup. But it was exciting to think about England as T20 pioneers, just like England had recently established themselves as ODI pioneers.

The primacy of judgement

By chance, just before becoming selector, I was fortunate to be sent a new edition of *A Guide to the Classics* by the English philosopher Michael Oakeshott (co-authored with Guy Griffith).

The title was an in-joke (very Cambridge *c.*1936) because the subject of the little book isn't Latin and Greek, but a classic horse race – the Epsom Derby. Griffith and Oakeshott imagined 1930s pupils appeasing their teachers by clutching a book which appeared to have a reassuringly lofty title, but was actually about how to decide on a good punt in a classic horse race. (The book's subtitle is 'How to Pick the Derby Winner'.)

This mischievous essay by two young academics is a rare example of brilliant thinking honing in on the question of selection in sport, almost by chance. Along the way, *A Guide to the Classics* does something much more. In plain, simple English it explains why all good decision-making relies on a sound approach to past evidence. The book is about how to think well about history in order to make superior (though never infallible) judgements.

A Guide to the Classics uses sporting performance as a prism for how to think about history. Oakeshott is grappling with the same questions of how to weigh evidence and make judgements – but all transposed on to the terrain of racing, distilled into a few dozen pages, and delivered in the mode of witty conversation. To which this former history undergraduate (who struggled through Oakeshott's densely argued *Experience and Its Modes*) responds: so why didn't anyone tell me about the short, funny and sporty version when I was reading the long, complex and serious one?

Oakeshott stressed that the job of the historian is to hone in on the most essential parts of the story. A complete history is not only impracticable but literally impossible; it would be unending. Real history, in contrast, 'requires imagination, not indeed to invent something that has never existed outside one's head, but the imagination that can help to reconstruct something that has really happened, from evidence that is not complete'.

That is the central point about history: while it deals in facts, it depends on interpretation. And the most important aspect of interpretation is the historian's judgement about *what* really matters. I wasn't seeking a proof, but instead an *inevitably approximate and incomplete* but still essential set of judgements about England's three teams.

What was essential in an account of England's all-round position that could be addressed and improved via selection? There was a need to get to the core of 'what was going on'. Future strategy could only follow from that.

In Tests, we needed to increase variety in the bowling unit to improve performance overseas; elevate the team's needs above individual preferences; maximise talent on the field even if it was assembled innovatively; and establish a wider pool of good players to cope with the increasing strains of a hectic schedule.

In ODIs, we should be on the lookout for one final injection of star power while also remaining mindful of the squad's existing strength of purpose and clarity of direction.

In T20s, I favoured being as innovative and aggressive in selection and strategy as England had been in their recent ODI form, nurturing England's next white-ball juggernaut.

But it was also obvious that these three strategies would sometimes be in tension with each other. A number of England's leading players belonged to all three teams simultaneously. There would be moments, given the relentless nature of England's schedule, when players would have to be rested from one format so they could be at their best for another – all the more reason, as a selector, to work hard on developing next-in-line players (what we call 'depth') to reduce dependency on our most precious assets. Overall, England's three formats needed to be studied and understood both individually and collectively. That was one of the most demanding aspects of a selector's job.

The first half of the book considers the questions and solutions we adopted in pursuit of resolving (or at least improving) the issues and challenges facing England's three teams in 2018.

How we fought against selection becoming cautious and conventional. How we looked for players who unlocked collective potential. Why innovation is so important – and so unpopular. How to build teams, not just rank individuals. And what data allows you to see and why it's so controversial.

The second half of the book explores the foundations that helped me to make sense of those challenges – conceptual frameworks, far out of sight from public discourse, that were central to my way of understanding and approaching decisions.

Your 'voice'. Staying free from drudgery. The ability to play with problems, not just 'work hard' at them. Standing back from the fray. The interplay of theory and practice. Remaining independent.

So this is a book of ideas, but it also draws significantly on personal experience, especially the three years with England cricket. I've always been interested in how ideas can improve performance in the 'real' world. That is one reason why sport has retained such a hold over me – as a player, a writer and a selector. Sport is a forum where ideas can be tested – with quick, truthful and impossible-to-fake feedback. It's called the wins and losses column.

In my time with England, I was lucky to work with some brilliant people – administrators, coaches, medics, psychologists and players. In any collaborative exercise, it is always hard to disentangle causes and contributions. That's why, as the book explores, it's better to think about successful teams rather than successful individuals.

Those three years with England – though the spell was certainly not without flaws and disappointments – were successful by objective measures.

From May 2018 to May 2021, across all three formats (Test, ODI, T20), England played 116 matches, winning 71, losing 36, with 9 drawn or 'no result'.

In spring 2021, the ECB decided to abandon its experiment of having a modern and fully independent selection process (including the role of National Selector). But the ECB's decision to abolish the system of selectors did have one accidental benefit: it provided a clear-cut ending and a corresponding sense of completeness. Something was started, tested and then closed down.

Three years is a decent sample size in sport. This book developed from immersion, then reflection: three years of thinking, talking, debating, feeling confident one minute and then sometimes unsure of the next move, weighing evidence, reconsidering propositions, balancing conviction with scepticism, thinking about analogies, testing theories, learning from mistakes – above all, making decisions.

The book is about how to approach decisions and what I've learnt by making them. It explores frameworks which I find helpful, though in writing it I learnt things that had never come together in quite the same way before. It felt like a discovery rather than a primer.

Decision-making in the real world is not – and cannot be – an exact science. It's about judgement – with reference to plenty of evidence, sometimes even some 'scientific' strands – but a judgement nonetheless. One of my aims is to restore the primacy and standing of judgement as a concept, and to distinguish it sharply from 'hunches' and 'punts' (though there is scope for those, too). It's unfortunate that mainstream debate about decisions and evidence is so often hollowed out into misleading cartoons: 'What the science says ...' on one side, versus 'taking a punt' on the other.

That is not to say that decisions don't benefit from the constant search for better sources of information and superior tools to make sense of that information. Even when the concept of a 'proof' is inappropriate, there are still better and worse ways of doing it. These were the options, this is the decision, here are the reasons.

But a decision-maker should be very wary of trying to dress up decisions about the messy and human world of sport as 'science'. As we all learnt during the same period – and references to Covid-19 will be as limited as possible – 'What the science says ...' can be a problematic formulation designed to absolve responsibility. Better to admit it: it's a judgement. Instead of hiding, we should come out in plain sight.

That's the spirit and mood of this book – open, sceptical and intimate. I'd like the reader to walk alongside me, as though we were just chatting it all through. As I often said to my colleagues in selection, there is clearly a place for meetings – and if we are going to have meetings, let's have good meetings – but there's nothing like conversation to explore ideas and pursue answers.

2
'Uninstitutional Behaviour'

I'm a pretty dispassionate watcher. But it would have been inhuman not to feel closely engaged at the start of play on 3 June 2018, as England took the field against Pakistan at Headingley. It was day three of the final Test against Pakistan and England had to win the match to level the series.

Defeat at Lord's in the previous game (my first Test match as selector) meant that the Test team had now lost six of their last seven games. How much longer would England fans tolerate a losing streak? Now, striding out to bat together in the 2nd Test at Headingley, were two new picks – with Sam Curran resuming on 16, playing his first match for England and celebrating his twentieth birthday that day, and Jos Buttler not out 34, back in the team after a long exile.

A few days earlier, Curran was a relative newcomer in the Surrey side, let alone thinking of England. He still didn't own a car. When I called him two days before the match with the news of his selection for England, the conversation quickly turned to the train timetable.

But late the previous evening, going out to bat on debut in fading light and the game in flux, Curran had instantly announced himself. A nonchalant pull for four, then next ball a glorious straight drive – a classy combination at any time, let alone in the first moments of a career. Buttler had also counter-attacked, with the prospect of batting with even greater freedom the next day.

Taken together, the mood set by Curran and Buttler set the tone for the whole summer – audacious, expressive and risk-taking, but also smart. Now, on the morning of day three, the two men punched gloves, as modern cricketers do, on the edge of the outfield before joining the Pakistan fielders out in the middle for the opening skirmishes.

Barely an hour later, Buttler had raced to 80 not out. His last 35 runs had come off just 11 balls – 4, 6, 1, 1, 1, 4, 4, dot, 4, 6, 4. That would constitute an incredibly fast scoring rate in a T20, let alone a Test match. (If he'd carried on at the same rate, he would have needed only seven more balls to reach his first Test century.) Buttler's last six was smashed over the bowler Mohammad Abbas's head, way over the boundary, landing deep in the building site at the far end of the ground. 'Nailed, absolutely nailed!' was the description on TV, 'nearly a conversion into the rugby ground'. The shot encapsulated the measured brutality of the whole knock.

England's innings closed with the crowd on its feet, optimism coursing through the ground – and through the veins of the England team. A win was no longer likely, it was certain. The ship had turned.

Six weeks earlier, I'd been sitting in my study, writing a history book. Now I was in the heart of an excited crowd, watching big decisions play out in front of me. Back in the real world.

Playing the ball where it lies

Here is a list of batting averages: 20, 27, 25, 16, 25, 28, 24, 28.

When I joined as chief selector, those were the career averages of the most recent eight specialist batters selected – and then dropped – by England. In Test cricket, averaging 40 – though it's a high bar – is considered the benchmark for a top player. So those eight career averages were all a long way adrift.

In other words, the previous eight players selected to bat for England in Test matches had a mean batting average of 24 – an extremely disappointing return. And yet a decent case could have been made for the selection of each individual player. So while the selections might have ended in disappointment, they weren't necessarily mistakes. The eight batters had been chosen by the selection panel of James Whitaker, Angus Fraser and Mick Newell and head coach Trevor Bayliss – all sound, sensible judges of cricket who were deeply committed to England winning. I was fortunate that I knew all the selectors personally and I respected them as a panel.

That helped with my understanding of the situation. World-class alternatives to bat at the top order for England were scarce to the point of non-existent (though obviously we would keep looking tirelessly). County cricket, for a variety of reasons that we will come to later, wasn't producing batters well suited to success at Test level. But reforming the structures of English cricket at the level below international cricket is not a selector's job. We had to live with the system and make the very best of the players who were available.

In the immediate term, what were we – what was I? – going to do about England's problems with the lack of batters to select?

The biggest problem wasn't the *ranking* of players (though you can always try to do better here, and we'll shortly come to some metrics that helped us) but *supply*. If players aren't there, even the best analysis can't find them.

Given the recent past – an extensive sample of new players who'd been tried out and discarded – the short-term answer would not reside in new data, but greater imagination. Data spelt out the problem, but in this instance data couldn't help much with the answer – other than, perhaps, providing us with a sense of freedom and licence to do things differently. Paradoxically, knowing the data, at this moment and in this context, liberated us from the shackles of hunting for fool's gold in the data.

Instead of selecting the next-in-line county batter, what if there was a different approach to fit England's current needs? I thought there was.

Suppose we accepted that England's talent was unevenly distributed and, to borrow a metaphor from golf, played the ball where it lay? OK, so England didn't have reams of new top-order batters to select. But what *did* England have? *All-round talent.* We had an over-supply of all-rounders – seam-bowling all-rounders (like Chris Woakes), spin bowler all-rounders (such as Moeen Ali, Adil Rashid and Dom Bess) and wicketkeeper-batters (Jonny Bairstow, Jos Buttler, Sam Billings and Ben Foakes).

If an all-rounder – who bats *and* does something else – gets more runs than a 'batter', then why persist, on principle (if principle is the right term) on picking the 'batter'? Like most useful questions, it was disarmingly simple. It was also anchored in the world as it is, not the world as you'd like it to be – which is another lesson that applies to teams in all contexts, beyond as well as inside sport: sometimes you have to make do with what you've got and apply your thinking there.

We had to discard unhelpful fantasies. We couldn't pretend players existed who did not exist. And that unpalatable fact could not be made to go away by thinking we could solve everything with a clever metric. Yes, we would work hard on making data from county cricket more useful. But it was a long-term project. And we had matches to win right now.

In the first couple of weeks in the job, I watched a lot of county cricket, live at county grounds and also via recorded footage on my iPad (I became pretty much addicted to watching next-in-line players). I also spoke to everyone – players, coaches, umpires and scouts – about who we could select to improve the team. (It's worth remembering, as the data analyst Nathan Leamon often used to say to me, that a good team can always be improved and a bad team can always be made worse.)

In all those many conversations, there was little common ground about new batters who were ready to be called up to the Test team. A variety of names cropped up, but there was little unanimity. Most people agreed that the stand-out young batter of his generation was Ollie Pope, the 19-year-old Surrey star. But Pope had never batted at one, two or three – which was where the gaps in the batting order were most likely to open up for England.

So I started asking everyone the same question: 'If you were captain of Pakistan or India [the two Test teams England were playing that summer] and England had just lost a wicket, which batter would you rather *did not* come out of the pavilion in an England shirt: either a) any of these new batters under discussion or b) Jos Buttler?'

Buttler, aged 28 and entering his prime, was an exceptional talent. He was already a world-class player for England in both

ODIs and T20 formats, where he was Eoin Morgan's trusted vice-captain and a significant part of the brains trust. Yes, there were complexities about considering selecting Buttler for the Test team. For a start, he wasn't in the country: he was at the Indian Premier League, playing for the Rajasthan Royals. He had been mostly on the outside of England's Test team for the last two and a half years and hadn't anticipated being brought home for the Pakistan Test series. But that was a question of logistics; I was more interested in ability. And Buttler was a unique match winner – what he was doing at that exact moment for Rajasthan Royals.

When I framed the Buttler question, it would usually prompt umms and errs and a sense of avoidance. Phrases would form along the lines of *compliance* rather than selecting winning teams. But he wasn't even playing red-ball cricket … but it wasn't the ideal signal about the strength of county cricket at the level below England … but how would this left-field decision be *presented* … but shouldn't we support the *usual path* into the Test team …

Occasionally, someone would cut straight to the point. Andy Flower, England's former head coach who had then become head of the England 'Lions' (England's 'second' or development team) answered plainly: 'The answer to your question, if I was captain of Pakistan, would have to be Buttler. Because you'd know that he can really hurt you.'

Much more often, however, my question was greeted with a classic bureaucratic reflex: it was all so very … *difficult* … wasn't there a less *controversial* move?

The bureaucratic machine

The investor David Swensen, who grew the endowment fund of Yale University from $1 billion to $30 billion, had an adage about the challenge of making decisions on behalf of an institution (my emphasis added):

> Active [investment] management strategies demand **uninstitutional behaviour** from institutions, creating a paradox that few can unravel.

This a central theme of the whole book. How can institutions resist thinking too much like institutions? How can a bureaucracy fight against the risk-averse tendencies of bureaucracies?

Because many teams are de facto bureaucracies – including the wider team I belonged to at England cricket. The ECB's cricket department – the people who are responsible for driving high performance across England's cricket teams – comprises more than 50 people (coaches, analysts, doctors, trainers, physios and so on). There's a whole England cricket machine.

Through little fault of the individuals involved, these organisational machines take on their own needs and habits – principally what suits the machine itself. This is the second meaning of 'machine' in this book. First, we need to remember the value of human judgement set against machine learning and algorithms. Second, now using 'machine' metaphorically, we need to emphasise the human dimension within the machine-like structures of the working world. Put simply, how effectively can human beings resist the slide into bureaucratic inertia?

Very few leaders today get to make decisions entirely independent of a machine. In sport, this dimension is relatively new. As recently as the early 1980s, cricket was basically a despotism – under the captain. Mike Brearley, probably the greatest Test captain in England's history, was mostly assisted by one team manager and one physio. The rest of the group were his players. This simplicity played to his strengths: as Brearley was extremely perceptive and deft, he was able to exert a positive influence in many areas of team life, areas which would now command dedicated professional roles. That creates an interesting counterfactual which I've discussed with him: if Brearley was leading a team today, his role would not only be smaller, it would also demand more management of the team's semi-permanent 'civil service' or bureaucracy. So managing the team's 'machine' would also consume his energy and resources – not just managing the players. And while this machine can be good at helping leaders to achieve things – if it agrees with you – the machine can also be effective at *stopping you* from doing things.

What you can't do, if you want to make effective decisions, is pretend the machine doesn't exist, or leave it to follow its own path of least resistance. The very existence of complex organisational structure, despite the wishful mission statements about 'vision' and decisiveness, cuts against executive clarity and dispatch. The machine, even though it was notionally designed by human beings to serve their ends, ends up being one of the principal factors most in need of managing and directing. The greater the number of limbs, the harder it is to move forward quickly and in a straight line.

So one of the most important gifts in this context is *organisational intelligence*: the ability to translate good ideas into institutional effectiveness. Ironically, this demands reminding people that they think better as individuals than they do when they start trying to think like an organisation.

As selector, I came to favour the question: 'What would you do if you were the *sole* decision-maker?' This was designed to stop people answering with compromise already priced in: 'Well, I guess we aren't going to, so I suppose we could ...' The compromises could come later. First: what do you think? What do you really think?

Owning risk

During a rain break at an early-season county match, I telephoned Buttler in India. It felt like a significant phone call. I never know exactly what I'm going to say in any conversation. (No one, surely, wants a conversation to feel so thought out that it feels almost scripted.) But I do think carefully about what I believe and how I'd like the other person to interpret the mood of the call. If my own thoughts are clear, I hope they come across truthfully and spontaneously during the conversation.

First of all, where was Buttler in his own head? Did he have ambitions to play Test cricket again? Yes, he did.

From my side, what did I want to convey? That I wanted to see him winning Test matches for England. Because I felt sure he could. I strongly believed in him and his ability. But I also made no promises about selection – he had a hand to play by staying in good form, and I didn't want to make any assumptions about the selection meeting the following week. Nonetheless, I was totally direct and truthful. I wanted all the players, not just Jos, to know that I was prepared to take risks and do what I believed in.

We'd speak in a week or so, I said. Stay in form. Keep having fun.

Over the next few days, Buttler completed a world-record sequence of scores in T20s: 67, 51, 82, 95 not out, 94 not out.

My appointment – for the time being – was the only change in the overall selection panel. Three selectors stayed on from the old four-man committee (there hadn't yet been time to go through the recruitment process for the second full-time selector).

So when we gathered for a selection meeting at the end of May to choose the Test squad to face Pakistan, I was far from sure how the meeting would pan out. I'd decided, quite far in advance, that I wouldn't try to over-manage the situation. The two outgoing selectors, Mick Newell and Gus Fraser, had given very good service to England cricket. And they'd both been extremely open and forthcoming with me as I found my feet. The best thing for England cricket was that they continued to make the case for the players they thought should be selected – even if that meant there was no guarantee that the selection meetings would be smooth or easy for me. Better honest debate than people double-guessing what I wanted.

The meeting was held at Lord's at 8.30 a.m. I'd stayed in London the night before, and was up just after dawn for a long walk in Regent's Park, thinking things through.

The room at Lord's comprised the four selectors (including head coach Trevor Bayliss), captain Joe Root, England MD Andrew Strauss, data analyst Nathan Leamon and the head of Talent ID Mo Bobat. Looking back, I can see how much I had to learn about running a meeting in those early days. But I was happy with the outcome. We added two new names to the squad for the 1st Test: Buttler (who was about to bat in an IPL match in India) and also the 20-year-old off-spinner and lower middle-order batter, Dom Bess.

Our decisions for the Pakistan series certainly turned attention towards selection. First, they confounded people who had believed that selection was immediately going to be placed in the hands of a heartless algorithm – clearly that wasn't the case. Second, selecting a player straight from the IPL was seen in some quarters as lining up with 'white-ball cricket' over 'red-ball cricket' in the age-old culture war about the soul of the English game. That was entirely untrue. I have reverence for the older format and it's deep in my blood. Yes, as an unintended consequence, the selection was a signal that the new selection system was unconstrained by the past. But the Buttler move was totally pragmatic. Given an unusual set of circumstances (including the talent distribution of the players), the motivation was very simple: to win cricket matches.

In the 1st Test, Buttler and Bess shared a partnership of 126 (albeit in defeat). In the 2nd Test at Headingley, Bess made another 49, and Buttler notched up his quick-fire 80 not out. Buttler was player of the series.*

Those early selections had my fingerprints on more than most decisions across my three-year spell as selector. Because in spring 2018 everyone knew I was the only newcomer to the selection panel. There was a peculiar thrill about the jeopardy of that early period, when I was more exposed and alone.

* Cricketing readers might point out that Buttler, after a dip in form in 2021–22, was dropped from the Test team. But the performance of the team during his period in the side remains intriguing. After being recalled against Pakistan, Buttler was selected for 39 Tests – with England winning 21, losing 13 and drawing 5. As a benchmark, in the 39 preceding Tests, England had won 14, lost 19 and drawn 6.

But that summer also presented the opportunity to drive forward the modernisation of selection through off-field recruitment. In July 2018 we found exactly the right person to complete the team – James Taylor. James would have been still playing for England himself if a heart condition hadn't ended his career three years earlier. James was 29, and we were England's youngest ever selectors. James was a superb colleague for the next three years: exceptionally knowledgeable about the modern game, honest and always great fun. We became our own team, a team based on trust and mutual respect. Crucially, James and I sometimes interpreted cricket through a different lens – we constantly debated past performance set against future potential – and those differences enhanced our overall partnership. To expand your own vision, you need to find people who can see things from a different angle.

As always, early decisions were revealing. What was the vision for the team's development? Was an authentic voice emerging? By the end of 2018, even our critics agreed that there had clearly been a departure from the old way of doing things.

Though there was no strict 'policy' uniting all the selections, there were some subtle signals. First, we backed young talent. Three players, Bess, Curran and Pope, made Test debuts aged 20 or younger. Second, we backed gifted players to bridge across formats without specific match preparation: first Buttler, then Adil Rashid. Third, though we introduced quite a large number of new players, very few players dropped out of contention altogether. Instead, we wanted an expanded pool of players so that the final XI could be more bespoke for the conditions, and also to help workload management in a very congested fixture list. Selections didn't have to be forever, players could – and should – come again. We wanted to keep talent in the fold, not banish it for good.

In summary: we wanted a squad of England players who (though not necessarily all young in age) believed their best days were ahead of them, who had class and ability, and who allowed us to assemble a balanced team to suit conditions anywhere in the world. Hopefulness, talent, adaptability.

In 2018, England rapidly climbed to second in the world rankings, powered by a sequence of eight victories in nine Tests – our second-'winningest' streak since England's first match in 1877. Quite a turnaround.

Perhaps the most intriguing pattern was the success of the newcomers. Player of the series against Pakistan: Buttler. Player of the series against India: Curran. Player of the series against Sri Lanka: Foakes. All three had just been introduced into the team – Buttler recalled, Curran and Foakes debuted.

All of which, perfectly understandably, added to the curiosity in the air: what was this new approach to selection? How were the selectors arriving at different decisions? In particular, did we now have different and better data? Was there a 'scientific' formula at work beneath the surface?

Perhaps we could have done a better job of explaining that there was both more and less to it than that.

Decision-maker not sinecure

England played a lot of memorable cricket during that Headingley Test match. But from a personal perspective, nothing topped an unexpected phone call I received during the first day's play. It came from the Director of Cricket at a county team who rang when Sam Curran was just settling into his debut. 'I'm sitting with two top county players who want to know from you how you've selected Sam Curran over them?'

I replied – I hope courteously – that this was because Curran had a much higher batting average than either of them and that Curran was also a left-arm swing bowler, which, last time I checked, they weren't.

Curran, as we will see in the next chapter, brought two different super-strengths: irrepressible all-round confidence and, critically, left-handed variety to our bowling attack. Overall, with the Curran selection, as with Buttler, I believed that taking a contrarian position brought value for the team. Put differently, the selections represented a *change from what otherwise would have happened.*

That is the job description. The point of diverging from conventional wisdom is not that you are trying to be clever. (Though I love the absurdity of the cliché 'too clever by half' as it implies that being less clever brings its own virtue.) Diverging from conventional wisdom is not a show-off position designed to draw attention to yourself. You are simply accepting personal risk by changing the status quo in the pursuit of improving performance.

The perceptive American investor Howard Marks tells a story about his own early career that applies to making judgements in all areas of life:

> At Citibank in the early 1970s, the senior-most panel, the Investment Policy Committee, would go off-site for semi-annual retreats. The high point consisted of voting on which industries' stocks would perform best over the coming year. It was my sense that if you added up the members' individual distributions, you'd get a summary distribution

that was pretty close to what would have been generated randomly.

In the same way, if a cricket selector (or selection panel) spent the whole time solely working out the *net average* of all the views held within English cricket and then making decisions that perfectly reflected and mapped this average of 'informed opinion', in that circumstance the value of that selector would be precisely ... zero! You wouldn't have a decision-maker or a thinker, but instead merely a pollster. And the job of the selector/pollster could be staffed out easily to an online polling company.

It is only when a decision changes the course of events that a decision-maker proves their value. That's why, to be useful, you have to do what you believe in, as with any great creative project. 'To make movies you need balls,' the film director Antonio Capuano announces in Paolo Sorrentino's *The Hand of God* (2021). And if the process isn't full of tension and struggle, you probably aren't doing it right.

The upcoming chapters will dig deeper into specific metrics we used and occasionally pioneered. Sometimes, we gained an edge here and we will explore how. But one day everyone will have the model you are using (another Howard Marks aphorism). So rather than hoping that an algorithm can negate the need to think for themselves, decision-makers need to stay close to the value only they can add. Your world view, your intuition, your confidence: that's the greatest part of your value.

If your decisions do not diverge from conventional wisdom in any important respect, you are failing to do your job. Indeed, you no longer have a job. You have a sinecure.

3
Swarm Harmoniser

A swarm harmoniser is something or someone that improves the collective output of everything around it. The term derives, via biology and physics, from studying the co-ordinated movement of groups of animals.

Liverpool FC's first Premier League title in 2019–20 was partly based on the approach of their analysis department: they wanted to find players whose movement and understanding of space contributed to the whole team performance, over and above what could be captured in terms of individual metrics. Liverpool were looking for swarm harmonisers.

In 2003, when David Beckham was bought by Real Madrid and the (then) underrated Claude Makélélé was sold by Real to Chelsea, Zinedine Zidane quipped: 'Why put another layer of gold paint on the Bentley when you are losing the entire engine?' With Makélélé, Real had won seven titles in three seasons. Without him, they went for three years without lifting *La Liga*. Every great team has its own underestimated contributor – exactly the kind of player who is easy to miss from a recruitment perspective: 'You need to spot talent that whispers,' in the phrase of Rasmus Ankersen, former Director of Football, Brentford FC, 'not just talent that shouts.'

If you think the concept of a swarm harmoniser sounds like a fluffy, friendly notion that lacks edge or real-world grit, think again. Sometimes it takes an independent-minded person, with different skills or a fresh approach (ideally, both), to make the whole function better. In fact, it is the point of difference that can provide a new-found collective serenity. Inevitably, the concept is context-dependent: each swarm requires a different harmoniser. If you are assembling a team, in any sphere, you'll need to work out who or what might make the whole thing function better – and then add it to the group as quickly as possible.

How's this for a sequence:

Won
Won
Won
Won
Won
Won
Won
Lost
Lost
Won
Won
Lost
Drew
Lost
Won

Won
Won
Won
Drew
Won
Won

That's 21 matches, 15 wins, two draws and four defeats. The list is the sequence of wins, defeats and draws in Test matches, in order, played by Sam Curran.

Why Curran got selected, and how the team did so well when he was there, are both revealing stories.

Two days before that 2nd Test match at Headingley, just as the pressure was bubbling up, we discovered at training that star all-rounder Ben Stokes was injured and likely ruled out of the match. Stokes brings so much more than just runs and wickets, and the team atmosphere looked clouded throughout net practice. In the air, the question was obvious: who should the selectors bring in instead of England's talisman Ben Stokes?

Under pressure, the easy thing to do is to seek a decision that offends no one. Stay under the radar. That isn't what we did. We went the other way.

There is never a good moment to see your pivotal player sidelined. But the Stokes injury prompted us to think creatively about bad news. Every selection is an opportunity. If that opportunity arises from the disappointment of injury, it's still an opportunity. Stokes's injury depleted our on-field star quality at a difficult moment. But it was also a chance to do something new, a chance to invest opportunity in a future talent – maybe someone who possessed something of Stokes's epic competitiveness, but with something different built in, too.

Now for three types of evidence: first personal experience, then data, and finally observation.

In 2007, I played on what has claim to be officially the flattest and easiest batting wicket in the history of first-class cricket. The game was at Taunton, between Middlesex and Somerset. More hundreds were scored in that game than in any other match, ever. A hundred, in other words, was the new normal. Almost everyone who was selected as a specialist batter got a hundred, including me. The opposition captain got a triple hundred. Bowlers also got hundreds, both in their bowling analysis and with the bat. Flat, flat pitch. When captaining the field, I felt I needed 20 fielders. And that still wouldn't be enough.

On the final day of this batting paradise, I found myself batting out for the draw. Somerset had a good bowling side, including the England bowler Andrew Caddick.

Caddick was one of the best bowlers I ever faced – with bounce, control, movement and enough pace. But even Caddick was rendered toothless on this feather bed. In fact, his pure and orthodox high action, in conjunction with such a serene and flat pitch, seemed to create a perfectly ordered compound effect. As an orthodox right-handed batter facing an orthodox right-arm bowler, it felt as though you almost couldn't get out. And this was facing Caddick, who could, in different circumstances, make you look stupid.

Then the left-handed swing bowler Charl Willoughby came on to bowl. For a moment, in my complacency, I forgot to reset the angle of my feet and stance. (Against a left-arm over-the-wicket bowler, a right-handed batter usually opens up his stance a little, splaying out his front toe a touch.) But I didn't, and even in such batting-friendly conditions, I managed to make a mistake and edge a catch to the slips. It went just between the fielders and landed safely. But then something strange happened. My Zen-like calm had been interrupted. Suddenly I was thinking about different angles, and making changes to my stance. I was fretting. The whole game now seemed to be about adjusting my positions according to the bowler. Fretting on the flattest pitch in history! I'd lost my rhythm.

Here is the really interesting thing about my experience at Taunton in 2007. Suddenly, I wasn't only playing badly against Willoughby, the left-armer. I was also batting badly against Caddick – which, only a few minutes before, had been easier than I'd ever known in my career. Moving between being lined up for a left-arm bowler and a right-arm bowler had taken me into a more effortful and stressful situation. One ball bowled by one left-arm bowler had changed the contours of the whole contest between bat and ball. The left-arm bowler, just by exercising his normal game, had made the right-arm bowlers better.

Left-handedness wasn't only an advantage to the left-hander himself, and hence to his team, through individual merit alone. By making others better, too, the left-hander had also made the whole bowling attack more potent.

I survived through to the close of play and completed, unheroically, the match's eighth century. But I learnt something much more interesting that would stay with me in other, more important contexts: the importance of variety in a team. It is variety – variety of archetypes – that helps to make a team more than the sum of its parts.

The science of lefties

In 2017, I wrote for the *New Statesman* about the advantages of being left-handed in sport. The German sports scientist Florian Loffing had recently collected and interpreted data on leading athletes across six sports (cricket, table tennis, tennis, squash, badminton and baseball) from 2009 to 2014. In sports which Loffing describes as 'fast-response', there is clearly a significant advantage in being left-handed. Only 10 per cent of the population is left-handed, but Loffing found that 30 per cent of major-league pitchers are lefties. The data supported what people suspect. Twenty-odd years ago, when I joined up with the New York Mets to write *Playing Hard Ball*, I was introduced to the American sports joke: 'If you're tall, you can get a job playing basketball. If you're left-handed, you can get a job in baseball.'

(As we will see later in the book, the same logic is now central to cricket's tactical frontier. This is the art of the 'match-up' in T20 cricket, by which analysts, coaches and captains try to engineer a dominant match-up at crucial points in the match. Similarly in rugby, a coach might orchestrate the necessary decoy runs that lead to a physical mismatch in a midfield tackle: he wants his strongest runner targeting the opposition's weakest tackler.)

The simplest factor at play here is that it is awkward for batters to adapt to the novelty of facing lefties. Batting techniques are predominantly built and honed in preparation to face right-armers. We are less effective against balls hurled at us left-handed. Given around 0.4 of a second (the reaction time in both cricket and baseball) to react to and then hit a ball travelling at close to 90 mph, adding an extra layer of challenge – the quirk of facing up to a leftie pitcher or bowler – makes an already difficult job even harder.

Experiments deepen our understanding of this effect. The reactions of elite athletes are largely intuitive and developed over decades of picking up 'cues' about where the ball is likely to go. When players in various sports watch video footage which is stopped at the point of release, they are worse at predicting where the ball will go from lefties than from right-handers.

The data analyst Nathan Leamon has now crunched the numbers on left-handedness in cricket. Seventeen per cent of seam bowlers in first-class cricket are left-armers, an 'over-representation' of 50 per cent. In Test cricket, left-arm seam bowlers collectively average 36.1 against right-handed batters and 35.6 against left-handed batters. Right-arm bowlers average 39 against left-hand batters and 37.1 against right-hand batters. Hence lefties 'lead' right-arm bowlers in both categories: against their own type, and against an opposite-handed opponent.

But there is another level of usefulness to left-handedness: in a collective endeavour, such as a bowling attack of five or six bowlers, left-handedness is a kind of swarm harmoniser. It makes the whole more effective.

Conversely, I'd witnessed the opposite situation play out – the absence of left-handedness (or an equivalent point of difference) – and it was still fresh in my memory. England lost the 2017–18 Ashes series 4–0. I was commentating for the BBC, so I watched the series carefully as a dispassionate observer. The Ashes were sealed in the 3rd Test at Perth. England selected four right-arm seam bowlers and a right-arm off-spin bowler – they used the same formation in each of the five Tests.

A case could be made for all five of those bowlers to be in the team on individual merit. But watching Australia amass 662–9, it felt as though Joe Root had only one line of attack, over and over again. As the bowling unit increasingly failed to stress the Australian batters, the pattern of the match became almost painful to watch. With each hour that passed, the dominance of Australia's batters became a kind of inevitability. One right-arm seamer, replaced by another, replaced by another. England were trying, I could see that, but they weren't able to get into the contest. Mitchell Marsh scored 181, nearly twice his next-highest career score. Take out that 181 and Marsh averages 22 as a Test batter. That is a measure of England's unvaried attack at Perth.

With those connected types of evidence in mind – the greater challenge created by a varied bowling attack, the advantages of left-handedness (demonstrated by ample data), and the problems of selecting too many bowlers belonging to the same archetype – let's return to an anxious England training ground at Headingley in 2018. Whom should we pick?

A case could have been made for several very decent county cricketers, all at the peak of their careers, all deserving, and none would have been criticised as a selection. But after perceptive input from Trevor Bayliss on the advantages of something new and different, we selected the 19-year-old Sam Curran to come into the squad as a replacement for Ben Stokes. For me, it was simple. Curran would bring variety to the bowling attack (genuine swing as well as a different angle), he batted with more flair and talent than some players who'd been selected as specialist batters, and he was a fresh, competitive voice who was unscarred by defeats or conservative attitudes. Curran ticked all three boxes that we needed.

At the very last minute, there was an attempt to change plans and (cautiously) recall an extra specialist batter instead of an all-rounder (Curran) for an all-rounder (Stokes). I kept making the same argument. In recent seasons, the last-picked specialist batter (a role that many players had been trialled in) had, all taken together, averaged not much more than 20 runs per wicket. If that was your rational expectation for a specialist batter, why play one? Curran would average at least that much as a batter alone. And, as a left-arm bowler, he would create the varied attack we craved. My argument was that what looked like a 'left-field selection' was actually sensible and strategic.

There was something else, too. Curran's character. I knew a lot about him, from his school days, from Surrey, from the England pathway. You never know how a debut will turn out. But I did know that Curran wouldn't be fazed.

On the morning of the match, with Stokes finally ruled out on fitness grounds, Joe Root named the starting XI, and Curran was handed his Test debut. Curran made a spirited contribution to the match, and overall England looked a fresher outfit, more capable of surprise and adventure.

It was in his second Test match that Curran showed his full hand. The match was at Edgbaston, the opening Test of the five-match series against the world's top-ranked Test team, India. Every aspect of the match was memorable from a selector's perspective: drama and controversy about selection in the run-up to the Test; a wonderful and fluctuating contest; and also the immediacy of the next difficult decision, immediately after the win.

Every time Curran entered the match, England had been in trouble.

First, as a batter, he made a handy 24 in a low-scoring 1st innings. Then, with India in a dominant position at 50–0 and well ahead in the match, Curran the bowler arrived in the contest. First, Curran swung a full ball into the right-handed Murali Vijay, who toppled over almost comically out of balance. Left-arm angle, significant swing, a new challenge; 50–1.

Then K. L. Rahul got his angles all wrong, chasing a wide ball that would have been hittable if it had been bowled by a right-armer. Rahul had failed to adjust his set-up in readiness for Curran's different line of attack – a feeling I remember well from hard-earned personal experience; 54–2.

Now it was Shikar Dhawan's turn to make the same mistake, flashing loosely outside off-stump; 59–3. Curran had all three England wickets, each one bound up with his archetype as a bowler, and the game was back on a knife edge.

India rallied to 148–5, perhaps getting their nose in front again. Then Joe Root brought back Curran, who did it again, producing a classic left-armer's wicket, with Hardik Pandya falling over an in-swinger.

That was the story of the whole series against India. The balance of power was always in flux, with Curran's interventions often tilting the contest in England's favour.

Player of the series

In terms of potential backlash and political risk, the squad for the 1st Test at Edgbaston was the biggest risk of the lot. Three Test matches in ... and we'd made big calls in all of them.

At Edgbaston, perhaps more than any other match, I felt I had to be present throughout, to give any support I could to the coach, Trevor Bayliss, and the captain, Joe Root. I wanted them to understand the deep sense of responsibility I felt for the selections we had made. Not just to hear me say the words, but to know the truth behind the words. Adil Rashid was now also back in the Test team having played no red-ball cricket for years; Jos Buttler, who had been in a similar situation a few weeks earlier, was now vice-captain of the Test team; Sam Curran, promoted so young and so quickly, was about to play the biggest match of his life. I was deeply invested.

And then my two-year-old daughter got sick with scarlet fever and was rejecting the antibiotics. My wife rang me from Suffolk, where she was spending a few days with friends. I got a series of trains across England to be with them, watching the cricket on my iPad. I lost count of how many people came up during the journey and asked, 'Shouldn't you be at Edgbaston?'

My daughter was already improving when I got there. The next day, after I had tried (and mostly failed) to be helpful, my wife reassured me that our daughter had turned the corner.

I eventually got back to Birmingham on the third day of the match, bedraggled and exhausted. By now, England had suffered a batting collapse and looked to be losing the Test match. We were 86–6 and Sam Curran was walking in to bat in an increasingly desperate situation. I'd forgotten my accreditation and couldn't go straight to the ground, but had to divert to the team hotel. I seemed outside myself, as if I had been watching myself live out the personal and private strands of my life with insufficient attention. Present but absent.

But it was back to the public role now. I needed to think clearly, and find the space and perspective to be ready for the game's aftermath.

The phone rang; it was my mum. 'Why aren't you at the ground?' Not a good start to the conversation, but it picked up thereafter. 'Sam Curran just hit a six off Ishant Sharma. Over extra-cover. Back foot drive. In-to-out over extra-cover. Tough shot.' Mum is steeped in cricket; her father, a canny Yorkshireman, played serious cricket. Mum explaining to me how hard it is to hit a fast bowler over extra-cover for six (a feat I've never achieved in my life) put a smile on my face.

I scrambled to the ground as quickly as I could. Curran made an audacious 63, with two towering sixes and a jaunty love of the contest. Curran the batter swung the 3rd innings of the match, just as Curran the bowler had swung the 2nd innings of the match.

By the final morning of the Test, having now recovered some equilibrium, I found myself sitting opposite Curran over breakfast at the hotel. He looked no more anxious or preoccupied than a talented sixth-former in the middle of a run of successful school games. Well played. Thanks mate. All in hand. Later that day, Curran finished an epic Test match as player of the match. The following month, England completed a memorable series victory over India in another classic Test match at Southampton. Curran, once again, transformed the match with fearless batting.

After the series win, I rang Joe Root to congratulate him. Had Joe been at all worried that India's batters might pull off the run chase at the end? Joe's answer was brilliant. He explained that, out on the field during the final innings, England possessed senior fast bowlers, brilliant all-rounders, an off-spinner, a leg spinner and a left-arm swing bowler … So, no, he'd never been worried – it was just a question of which wicket-taker was going to make the breakthrough.

It was an almost perfect summary of what I believed in – a full house of wicket-taking options.

The following week, I caught up with India captain Virat Kohli at the Oval match. I'd worked with Kohli at Royal

Challengers Bangalore during his record-breaking IPL season in 2016. Virat invited me into the India lunch-room and we chatted through the whole series. He paused for dramatic effect at one point, beaming with competitive recognition. England, he said, had played with such bravery in the big moments. Especially Curran.

After that game, Curran was named player of the series.

'Objectively'

To some extent, this book doesn't follow behavioural economics all the way, for all the useful lessons it has taught us. I don't think all 'biases' should be classified as 'mistakes'; it's not always hubris to believe in judgement; besides, if you always wait till you have sufficiently robust data, then the moment of the decision may well have passed. We often have to make do, operating with the double challenge of imperfect information and real-time pressure.

But I've certainly seen genuine biases (in other words, biases that *do* cause outright mistakes, rather than biases which are coping mechanisms) play out inside elite sport. One of the commonest problems is that decision-makers are swayed by things that make them feel good. Decision-makers tilt, often unknowingly, towards the convenient, the expedient and also, just as problematically, towards decisions that feel justified by the sweat and effort of the players they are observing.

There is a bias in sport towards the appearance of trying hard at practice. And at first glance, Curran can look a bit diffident. If you're not paying attention, you might think he has a cruisy attitude to life. Floppy fringe, informal but assured style, laid-back body language: you could be forgiven for thinking he was taking a surfing trip on a gap year between school and university. Curran is also short for a seam-bowling all-rounder (5ft 9). And he's not a particularly fast bowler – low 80s mph rather than some of his colleagues, who hit the low 90s.

But Curran plays matches better than he practises. It's the game – the thrill of the contest – that bring out his boldness in big moments. Curran belongs to a very small category of sportspeople to achieve instant success as he's moved up the levels. He was player of the match in just his second Test match. He was also, the following winter, player of the match in his second IPL match. That's an unusual double.

How do we judge people? By what they do when it matters most? Or how they go about their everyday business? Some coaches, in my opinion, can be too influenced by what they see at practice – perfectly understandably. There is a natural impulse at play. Coaches 'own' the practice ground. It is their domain and they like practice to look brilliant – organised, purposeful, muscular. When players pour every drop into practice, it makes coaches feel good – and look good.

Though I, too, am fascinated by skill acquisition and education – both my parents and three of my grandparents were teachers and I carried on university teaching throughout my time as selector – I was unusual for a decision-maker in modern sport because I've never been a professional coach. Perhaps, as one voice among a broad mix of opinion-makers, that diversity brought advantages.

There is a wide spectrum among top athletes in terms of practice versus performance. For some players, practice and its rituals are a central part of their professional identity – they love practice as much or more than games. For others, a certain amount of practice is clearly essential, but the heart of the matter is when the curtain rises and the match begins. They are performers.

As a selector, I did watch practice. But I didn't obsess over it or let it influence me too much. Everyone practises differently, and cricket is closer to golf in terms of classification than it is to rugby union. Batting and bowling, at the moment when they really matter, are entirely individual skills. Players have to learn how to make practice work for them.

At practice, you wouldn't always discern the fierce competitiveness inside Curran. One top coach said to me about him, 'Objectively, when I watch him at practice, I don't think he looks outstanding. But looking just at facts and figures in matches, he does very well.' The interesting word in that sentence is 'objectively'. Observations at practice, though they have value, are in fact *subjective*, performance data is *objective*.

Johan Cruyff, despite being the most influential coach in football history, admitted: 'Practice, I don't understand. Football, I understand that.' A connected point is that it's not always a good trait to find practice fulfilling per se. 'Choose a lazy person to do a hard job,' argued Bill Gates, probably partly for effect, 'because a lazy person will find an easy way to do it.'

Cruyff, the ultimate 'uninstitutional' thinker, also understood the way a team must fit together, and that an individual player's real impact on the whole is not always superficially obvious.

At the moment, Curran has an individual Test career bowling average in the early 30s. Very decent, but not stellar. But a bowler with variety can help those around him: when a batter has to move between different types of challenge, he's more likely to make a mistake. (Fast bowlers, for example, perform better statistically when there is a spin bowler in the side.)

Stuart Broad, an all-time great bowler, has an excellent overall Test bowling average of 28. But with Curran playing in the team, Broad has taken 65 wickets at an even better average of 21.

James Anderson, England's greatest ever bowler, has a career average of 27. When Curran is also selected, Anderson has taken 64 wickets at 19.

Combined, Anderson and Broad's bowling average improves by one-third with Curran in the team.

And England's win–loss ratio as a Test team when selecting Curran: 79 per cent.

4
The Shock of the New

As soon as you step off the playing field, argued Michael Lewis, writer of books on both sport and business, professional sport is less a business and more a social club:

> The Club includes not only the people who manage the team but also ... many of the writers and commentators who follow it, and purport to explain it ... The greatest offence a Club member can commit is not ineptitude but disloyalty.

The form of this unforgivable 'disloyalty' is often philosophical/strategic rather than personal. The club doesn't like disloyalty to its opinions, especially convenient and conventional opinions. One way of thinking about this club is as it being like a guild or establishment. There's a way things have always been done before, and that suits insiders all too well. Collectively, this manifests itself as implacable conservatism – which in turn brings extra risks for anyone who dares to try out new ideas.

Simply, innovation is one of the most impolite things you can do inside sport. And wherever new ideas are attempted, a backlash (often led by the tribal elders) can be guaranteed. So while innovation initially relies on clarity of perception, it stands or falls on courage and resilience.

Innovation typically involves a return to first principles. It begins with an insight. Insight in this context may be defined as an act of imaginative penetration yielding a non-obvious (or non-dominant) solution to a problem.

In sport, insight is the first domino, the quality that the most influential coaches and strategists possess above everything else. They see the game in an original way, allowing them to perceive – in ways that others cannot – how winning happens.

Daryl Morey, GM at the Houston Rockets then the Philadelphia 76ers in the National Basketball Association (NBA), inspired a revolution in basketball with devastating simplicity: increasing the proportion of 3-point shot attempts in relation to 2-point attempts. In 2017–18, the Rockets became the first team to play a season with more than 50 per cent 3-point attempts. Soon, everyone was catching up. As recently as the 2015–16 season, only six (out of 30) NBA teams took 3-pointers in more than a third of their attempts. By 2020–21, 28 teams were doing it.

As usual, the 3-point strategy had emerged at the level below the NBA, at the Rio Grande Vipers (owned by Morey's Houston Rockets) under the coaching of Nevada Smith. 'People definitely thought we were nuts and ruining basketball,' Smith reflected, 'and now it's the most widely accepted way to play.'

'Accepting a negative metric'

The shift towards 3-point shots had broad consequences for overall basketball tactics. But without the original and founding insight – that the game had been *too cautious in accepting the increased risk of missing* the shot altogether – there would have been no great leap forward.

'Whenever someone innovates in business or in life,' argues the poker player Caspar Berry, 'they almost inevitably do so by *accepting a negative metric* that other people are unwilling to accept.' (My emphasis.)

Morey's basketball teams were prepared to accept the negative metric of missing a higher proportion of shots – in return for higher value from the shots they did make.

Ajax and Holland's football teams in the 1970s accepted a different negative metric: they were prepared to live with *less specialisation across positions*. Wasn't it rational, asked captain Johan Cruyff and coach Rinus Michels, to have fewer players who could only do one thing (head the ball, hoof the ball, tackle hard), and instead more players who were all skilful and adaptable, switching positions throughout the match and expanding creative opportunity? Clearly this was possible. 'Total Football' showed how. With new freedom, however, came new responsibilities. 'When I saw [Wim] Suurbier going forward, I knew I had to go back,' the Ajax player Sjaak Swart reflected. 'I didn't have to be told. Everyone knew what to do.'

What began as perception about interchangeable positional play prompted a permanent and fundamental shift within football, from the individual to the collective. One genuine insight can inspire much wider possibilities, the theme of Chapter 6, 'Lego'.

My favourite formulation of 'Total Football' actually preceded its emergence by a decade and was written in an entirely non-sporting context. In 1961, the historian Arnold Toynbee – reflecting on the boundary walls that we impose on different academic disciplines – argued for the dismantling of these traditional divisions. He imagined a different, far more fluid intellectual framework,

> not like a Western house, but like a Japanese house, in which the internal arrangements can be given any number of alternative configurations, interchangeable at a moment's notice, because the interior is divided by screens, not by walls that are 'permanent fixtures'.

That is the essence of 'Total Football', the key to the transformation of the modern game.

Football's perennial distrust of innovation is a recurring theme of Michael Cox's absorbing history of tactics, *Zonal Marking*. Even the greatest strategists face a battle against the forces of conservatism. Arrigo Sacchi created a definitive and winning team at AC Milan, but moving away from the ultra-defensive Italian *catenaccio* ('lock-down') was 'considered an affront to Italian traditions ... he was almost considered a traitor'.

Every significant step forward in the evolution of football tactics has been met with the same response: they are 'reinventing the wheel', they are 'too clever by half', they are 'overcomplicating a simple game' and they 'don't understand what makes us who we are'. ('We' here could be anyone – the English, the Italians, the Spanish, the Portuguese ...)

Between 2008 and 2012, Spain's football team won two Euros and one World Cup – a hat-trick of the biggest global football events. They did so without, in some instances, selecting a striker. Normally the striker is the most famous player on the pitch, but Spain instead opted not to have one at all. This system – the 'False Nine' – was often ridiculed, right up to the Euro 2012 final. Famous English pundits routinely wondered, with a tone of baffled exasperation, how good Spain could really become *if they would only select a good strong lad up front to bang the goals in.* 'Spain's play is like love without the sex,' said Bixente Lizarazu, the former France defender.

In the final against Italy Spain won 4–0, making you wonder just how much sex Lizarazu thinks should accompany love. The opening goal looked pretty sexy to me – Xavi, to Iniesta, to Fabregas, to Silva, slinky passing all the way (metaphor ends here).

An early irony within the triumph of the highly skilful and anti-brutish Spanish model – a model which has since been devoutly imitated all over the world – is that it was initially highly controversial at home, too. It was deemed intrinsically unsuited to Spanish footballing temperament and culture. In 1998, the veteran coach Luis Aragonés urged Spain to be more Spanish (by which he meant less enamoured by touch and skill): 'Every country has its way of living football … and Spain has ours too. Spanish football has never been exquisite and we should not try to go against our DNA … We are not that kind of football team.'

And yet when Aragonés was then appointed as Spain's manager, he promptly changed his mind, selected lots of the players who he'd said couldn't all play in the same team – and the team won Euro 2008. This is a classic pattern of innovation:

erstwhile critics of new ideas, when they become persuaded of them, usually then carry on as if their initial position had never existed.

Football history, however, as Cox draws out, also refutes the facile notion that two similar players can't line up in the same team. Both the most successful club side of the last 20 years, and the most successful international team – Barcelona and Spain – determinedly lined up with two midfielders, Xavi and Iniesta, who were initially regarded as 'too similar' to play in the same starting XI. As Xavi recalled: '"We can't play together!" When you look back on that debate now, you think, "My God!" They had said the same about Pep [Guardiola] and me when I first came through … they said we didn't defend, we didn't fit in the same midfield, blah, blah, blah.'

Xavi and Iniesta were indeed similar – and, in tandem, supreme. Both Spain and Barcelona were built around their axis of talent and understanding. The national and club teams backed ability and class to overcome conservative resistance – and won big doing it their way.*

Of course, the cottage industry of anti-innovation extends wider than sport. The science writer Matt Ridley describes the classic features of opposition to change:

> An appeal to safety; a degree of self-interest among vested interests; and a paranoia among the powerful … How hansom cab drivers furiously denounced the introduction of the umbrella; how obstetricians long rejected the use of anaesthesia during childbirth; how musicians' unions

* From 2000 to 2021, Spain won 193 out of 281 matches, the 'winningest' team in football history.

> prevented the playing of recorded music on the radio; how the Horse Association of America for many years fought a rearguard action against the tractor; how the natural-ice harvesting industry frightened people with scares about the safety of refrigerators.

In sport, anti-innovation can be even more emotional. For many club members, innovation seems like a professional attack on their own personal narrative, the reassuring faith that 'what worked for me' must also, conveniently, be a universal truth.

Innovation vs ingenuity

There is an important distinction to be made between innovation and ingenuity, two deceptively similar concepts which we often confuse: 'He's an ingenious and innovative coach.'

While they *can* coexist, they are perhaps best understood as two distinct ways of solving a problem, two paths to the same peak, if you like. With innovation, derived from the Latin *innovatus* ('made new'), the nature of the game itself is altered. With ingenuity, the same cards are present and the same rules apply, but the hand is played better.

Johan Cruyff was an innovator; Jose Mourinho is ingenious. Sir Clive Woodward was an innovator; Eddie Jones is ingenious. Mike Brearley had an original conception of how to see the whole cricket match; Ray Illingworth was canny and shrewd. As a player then thinker about cricket, Martin Crowe was innovative; Javed Miandad was ingenious.

It is therefore not surprising that the fiercest critics of innovation are often the most personally ingenious. Perhaps ingenious operators feel genuine bafflement that any new tools could be required at all – after all, they achieved success without them.

Rasmus Ankersen's point about organisations – 'innovation normally happens one level down from the top' – also applies to individuals. With the exception of Cruyff (whose level of original insight matched the genius of his play, 'Edison and the lightbulb in one', in Simon Kuper's phrase), real innovation in sport usually depends on thinkers who were in some sense frustrated or thwarted as players.

Billy Beane, architect of the Oakland As story, never fulfilled his potential as a player and turned the experience into imaginative fuel; Bob Woolmer, pioneer of modern cricket strategy, had been an underrated player in an England shirt; Clive Woodward, never quite central to England rugby on the field, came back with a new blueprint as a World Cup-winning coach.

Even Guardiola, despite a wonderful and decorated playing career, felt his own skilful type of footballer was trapped on the wrong side of history as football became more physical and prescribed. 'I think players like me have become extinct,' he said in 2004, 'at most clubs players are given specific roles, and their creativity can only exist within those parameters.' That dissatisfaction with football's direction of travel spurred Guardiola, when he became a manager, to redefine the whole game in his own image.

Returning to Michael Lewis's 'Club' analogy, the problem facing many of its members is that they usually spend their whole professional and social lives talking to other club members, and listening deferentially to the best players in the club. This blinds them to the good ideas bubbling up just outside the clubhouse, where perception and insight are sharpened by restlessness with the status quo – all of which, inevitably, is the essential precursor for doing things differently.

Voluntary restrictions

On 16 February 2020, South Africa made a massive 1st innings score of 222 in the T20 match against England in the series decider.

England, remarkably, cruised over the line with five balls to spare, extending a sequence of five T20 series undefeated. Eoin Morgan, unselfishly batting lower in the order, smashed seven sixes in the win. At the top of the order, England's ultra-aggressive line-up had set the tone. Jonny Bairstow and Jos Buttler, batting at numbers two and three, scored a combined 121 runs off just 63 balls.

England's 226 was the second highest total in their T20 history. Out of the full 148 matches (stretching back to the first T20 game in 2005), three of England's four highest totals have come since 2018. Chasing down 222 at a canter wasn't just another win, it was confirmation of a thrilling direction of travel.

T20 is a game of restrictions:

- Each batting team is restricted to 120 balls (20 overs). The batters line up in any order the captain chooses and are allowed to bat for as long as they are able before being dismissed (or finish not out at the end of the 20 overs).
- Fielding sides are restricted in their placement of fielders – only two fielders are allowed outside the inner circle for

overs 1–6, and only five are permitted outside the inner circle from overs 7–20.

- Fielding captains are restricted in each bowler's allocation: each bowler is permitted 20 per cent of the full bowling innings (4 overs out of 20).
- Time is restricted – the fielding side must complete 20 overs inside a set time or face penalties.

You may have noticed a major asymmetry in the game's structural restrictions: where bowlers are restricted to 20 per cent of the team effort, batters are not. This point is painfully obvious and yet often overlooked.

The only central component of the game that is unrestricted is how a team chooses to divide and break up the 120 balls of each batting innings. Unlike with bowling – when the star bowler's exposure is limited to four overs – in batting, hypothetically, the same batter (if he scored a single or a three off the sixth ball of all of the first 19 overs) could face all 120 balls of the team innings himself, precluding any other batter from facing a single ball.

This is fundamental to understanding T20. Your best bowler is capped at using one-fifth of your resources. Your best batter is free to dominate the whole innings. Of course, as we all know, batting with the level of risk that T20 demands makes surviving through the whole innings very difficult, even batting for 60 balls out of the available 120 balls. But strictly in terms of playing regulations, the potential is there.

The essence of T20 is searching for the best solutions to restricted opportunities *intrinsically imposed on you by the format.* And yet it is commonplace for teams to restrict *voluntarily* their best batters' opportunity to shape the game – when coaches and captains bat them too deep in the batting order. It's a way of making a hard game even harder.

These are recurring memes to justify the approach:

> 'Yes, he's the best player across the whole innings, but the gap between him and the next-best player is wider in the context of the end of the innings than at the beginning of the innings ...'

> 'Yes, he's a great player, but we've got other players who are pretty good at the top of the order but fewer who are outstanding at the end ...'

> 'Yes, he's a great batter, but we don't want to use him high up in the order because we need him at the end to finish the match off ...'

All these arguments are routinely presented as just reasons for holding back brilliant batters until the game is often well on the way to already being decided. (Remarkably, sometimes the reasons are endorsed by the brilliant batters themselves. A. B. de Villiers, 'Mr 360', who stretched the contours of modern batting, often preferred to bat at number four in T20s, perhaps because he felt he could win any game from any position.)

As a rejoinder, here's a thought experiment. Imagine having the best bowler in the world in your side. And that you were permitted to bowl him not just for four overs but for 10 overs out of the 20. In this thought experiment, your star bowler would be allowed to bowl every single over from one end. And now imagine that, of your own volition, you made the strategic decision to hold back the best bowler in the world until the last few overs of the innings. Forget the beginning of the innings, when the tone is set and the foundations are laid. Forget the middle of the innings, when the contours of the final phase are shaped and teed up. No – we are saving the star bowler until the very end, only bowling him at the closing stages of the innings. Because the end of the innings is deemed to be very important (it is, after all, when the result is revealed in victory or defeat).

If those were the laws of T20, adopting this tactical approach for a champion bowler would be considered total madness. What about taking wickets up front? Why not bowl him across the whole innings? Why leave it so late? Why not maximise a superiority available to you for as long as you are permitted?

And yet, when presented with the inverse arrangement – the possession of an exceptional batter and the legitimate right of giving him access to the whole batting innings – many teams make all of the arguments that are quoted above.

But the case for superior players having access to maximum opportunity is rationally irresistible. It's not much use having a brilliant batter finish off the match if it's *already too late for him to finish it as a win.*

T20 strategy is like thinking in bets. The scale of the bet is the amount of opportunity invested. As a fielding captain, if you bowl someone for their full allowance of four overs, you are taking the biggest position backing that player. It's the same with the batting order. The biggest stake you can place on a batter is to give him access to the full 20 overs (120 balls).

England moved exactly in this direction in early summer 2018. The fast-scoring Jos Buttler moved up to open the batting, and powerful Jonny Bairstow (who'd often missed out on T20 selection) enjoyed spells at number three and number four. On the flip side, England Test captain Joe Root – highly skilled but less powerful – moved first out of the top 3, then completely out of the T20 side.

This was very tough on Root, who played superbly in the preceding T20 World Cup. Root, many sensible judges reflected, was 'too good' to leave out of *any* England format. Others argued that England had 'so many other options at opener', so why 'waste' a potential 'finisher' (that is, Buttler or Bairstow) in that position. Another objection was that England were 'breaking up' the ODI formula (when in fact it was a radicalisation of the ODI formula).

However, across the four years since those changes, England's T20 form has been exceptionally strong – in fact, unrivalled. By doubling down on its ultra-aggressive batting formation and approach, England's T20 team has been another example of Eoin Morgan leading an innovative and winning outfit.

Inevitably, returning to Caspar Berry's concept of the 'negative metric', there are times when it doesn't work. For England's T20 team, in being prepared to elevate the most destructive players to the top of the order, that sometimes means missing out on their ball-striking prowess at the end of the innings – exactly the part of the match everyone remembers with greatest clarity. In the same way, Pep Guardiola, who accepts a negative metric by packing his teams with skilful midfielders rather than 'outright' strikers, sometimes misses the presence of a player whose entire focus is goal-scoring rather than goal-creation.

Yet it is also true that Manchester City have won four of the last five Premier League championships, and England's T20 side, as I write, are ranked number one in the world.

And it's easy to forget – when you watch England smashing the ball to all parts in a T20 – just how much 'noise' and criticism the ultra-aggressive approach attracted along the way

– exactly as was the case with Spain's fast-passing football, and the Rockets' shooting for three points.

Once these strategies started to work, the debate simply shifted elsewhere, with sceptics becoming converts. This trend is another injustice awaiting anyone who is in the business of generating new ideas. When the ideas don't succeed, they stick in everyone's memories. But when the ideas do succeed, they become self-evident. (The same point applies to risks about selecting new players in general: selections that work become 'obvious' – only after the fact, of course – and therefore not worthy of credit. Selections that don't work become obviously wrong, inviting howls of disapproval.)

5
Super Over

As captain, you've got to keep talking to the bowler on the field, in good times as well as difficult times. Because if you only ever walk up to the bowler to talk when there is a crisis, he sees you coming and thinks, 'Uh-oh, here comes the captain. It's definitely a crisis.'

That was the gist of a conversation with Eoin Morgan after a selection meeting a year before the ODI World Cup of 2019. It was typical of Eoin's thinking and methods: to take the stress out of a situation, you have to normalise it. There is enough stress within sport at the best of times; communicating honestly with each other shouldn't add another layer.

Such a personal insight might seem an odd way to start a chapter significantly about data. But this chapter argues that however useful the data might be, there is, once again, no escaping the human dimension. Data shows things; people do things.

In England's 2019 World Cup win, statistical analysis and the human dimension were tightly interwoven – from the beginning of the journey in 2015 until the final denouement four years later.

'It's *so* on a young man'

A hundred overs, 600 balls, nine hours, from drizzly grey to golden evening light ... and still a dead heat – England vs New Zealand, the World Cup final of 2019.

And, in line with his general principles, Eoin Morgan is chatting lightly with his key bowler at a big moment, in fact the biggest moment. It is a beat before 7.30 p.m., and the low, late sun of high summer is almost directly in Jofra Archer's eyes as he stands at the top of his run-up. He knows he must bowl six good balls – and protect 15 runs – to win the World Cup.

But for the time being, Barbados-born Archer is just flicking a spinning white cricket ball in his hands. It's one of Archer's habits, however big the moment, like a kid enjoying his own dexterity just for the fun of it.

Flick, catch ... guess I've got to bowl in a second ... flick, catch ...
Could be any second.
Ready now, running in fast.
Bowling even faster.

In north London 28,000 fans are watching in a near-delirious emotional state. You can see that many are wildly entranced; 'gone'. Fifteen minutes earlier, it looked like England couldn't win. Ten minutes earlier, it looked like England couldn't lose.

For most of the day you had no clue either way. To gauge the emotional richness of the final, the crowd is a true barometer. The Lord's crowd can be understated to the point of outright reserved. Not this time. It found its primal roar.

When Archer is flicking and spinning the ball, the TV broadcast is at peak, with 8.92 million tuned in across the UK. (The World Cup final was the first England match on free-to-air TV in the UK since 2005, the perfect way for the game to return to mainstream: showing the greatest ODI of all time.) Around the world, 1.6 billion people are watching Archer.

Live on air, the former New Zealand cricketer and commentator Ian Smith sounds sceptical about Morgan's trust in the young star bowler: 'It's *so* on a young man ... it's a *big* call.'

World Cup, Jofra Archer, *big call*. We should have guessed it would end something like this.

Experience takes many forms

Wind back three months, to our selection for the World Cup.

Archer's qualification for England would only be confirmed in March 2019, the very brink of our time frame for tournament selection.

Should England leave alone the team that was breaking records and thrilling crowds? Or should we find space for a brilliant talent who strengthened England's few areas of need?

That question, among the many controversial subjects in the new selection panel's first 12 months, inspired the greatest interest.

Jofra has only ever held a British passport, but he grew up in Barbados and was part of the Barbados cricket pathway before joining Sussex and qualifying for England. As a bowler he has the full hand: pace, effortless technique, high release point, disguise (no one sees his bouncer coming), control, variety, intelligence, star quality and the ability to master new tricks quickly. He is one of the great talents in the game, and even back in 2019, before he'd played a single international match, Jofra was the talk of the cricketing world.

While ranked number one in the run-up to the tournament, England weren't flawless. As a bowling side, there were times when we needed more venom with the new ball. And a 'banker' for the death overs always gives a team extra confidence it can defend a total against the odds. If one player could combine those two qualities, the jigsaw would be complete.

There were many dimensions to the decision.

It was true that Jofra had played only fourteen 50-over matches before the World Cup – marked inexperience, some pundits argued. But he had played lots of T20 cricket, much of it against world-class opposition and under serious pressure at the Indian Premier League.

Jofra was already well known to some members of the World Cup squad. He was teammates with several England players at the Rajasthan Royals. And Jofra's innate confidence and X-factor were unmistakable. In the run-up to the World Cup, I caught up with Eoin Morgan at a Middlesex–Surrey match at the Oval. The thing about Jofra, Eoin reflected, is that he always seems to have the ball in his hands when the match is being decided. That was a prescient observation.

Crucially, we knew the exact pattern of Archer's performance in white-ball cricket because he'd played so much at the IPL (where every match is televised). As a result, Jofra's early career had not only been unusually public, it was also unusually data-rich. That's because televised games come with the added bonus – from a selector's perspective – of HawkEye data.

HawkEye is ball-tracking technology that is used in the Decision Review System (DRS), which must be available for all televised matches. Under this system, on-field captains are able to challenge on-field umpiring decisions, with DRS acting as the final judge and arbiter.

For example, in deciding whether a batter should be given out LBW, the on-field umpire has to make a judgement about whether the ball would have *gone on* to hit the stumps, if the ball had not first hit the batter's body.

If a captain disputes an on-field LBW decision, HawkEye – drawing on many high-definition cameras at the ground which are tracking the ball's path and trajectory – is able to reveal (with greater than 99 per cent accuracy) whether the ball would indeed have gone on to the hit the stumps and so whether the on-field decision was right or wrong. HawkEye tracks where the ball would have gone if its initial trajectory had continued. Instead of being an umpire's best guess, HawkEye is close to a dead certainty.

But the same data used to resolve umpiring decisions has other uses – and is of great value when it comes to analysing the game with unemotional clarity.

In order for HawkEye to predict whether the ball would have gone on to hit the stumps, it has to know the variables:

- Where was the ball released from (the bowler's 'release point')?
- How fast was the ball travelling?
- How much was the ball deviating from a straight line as it travelled?

- How much bounce was the pitch offering?
- How much was the ball spinning?

HawkEye 'wants' to answer these questions for a narrow purpose: arriving at the correct umpiring decision.

But a cricket selector also wants the answers to these questions for a much broader set of reasons: because they provide granular detail about how the game is being played and the quality of individual performances. 'How fast do you reckon he's bowling?' is one kind of question. 'Tell me from HawkEye data exactly how much speed this bowler has dropped off since getting tired in his sixth over?' – is a very different kind of question. In other words, where there are television cameras, there is also much better performance data. Having HawkEye data is like seeing cricket with X-ray clarity. Back to Archer: these circumstances made his career an unusual case. Normally when a player is being considered for England selection, a significant amount of the evidence is drawn from county cricket, where the data is far sketchier (as relatively few county matches are televised). But Archer's early career had been played out, to a remarkable degree, largely in televised games. As a result, we had both quantity and quality of evidence.

At the 2019 IPL, Archer had been the leading overseas fast bowler in the tournament by a number of metrics. He was also the second-fastest of any bowler (averaging 144 kph, with a high of 151 kph). And he was also outperforming all other England bowlers at the IPL. If you're going to make a 'huge call', it's nice to have rich evidence on your side.

I've often argued that the job of a selector is to take positions but not to make predictions. However, occasionally the rule is broken. At a selection meeting before the World Cup, the selection and data team felt strongly enough to slip into prediction mode: Jofra not only merited selection in the squad, but also in the final XI. Further, not only did he command a place in the XI, he'd also be England's leading fast bowler in the competition.

The most important question is often not 'What is the data saying?' but instead 'How much confidence do we have in the data?' and 'Is this the right question?' The foundational skill is understanding the *type* of information feeding into a decision. Are you making a 'best guess', or something more scientific? What kind of information is at your disposal? What is the extent and limitation of your knowledge?*

That's why all decision-making is informed, consciously or not, by a theory of knowledge. In sport, decision-makers might boggle at the term 'epistemology' – who doesn't? – coaches and selectors are all students of it, after a fashion. How do we know what we know? When you get into genuine debate with smart people inside sport about players – how good is he really? how do we know? – very quickly, beneath the surface, you find that you are arguing not just about sport, but also about knowledge itself. That's also why I found decision-making in cricket so interesting. All the time, without being able to avoid it, we were constantly revising how we gathered, assembled and weighed information. And asking how much we *trusted* that information.

In the case of Jofra Archer, we felt the evidence stood on very, very firm ground. I tried to give nothing at all away in the months before the World Cup, because whatever you thought

* The physicist Richard Feynman put it like this: 'Statements of science are not of what is true and what is untrue, but statements of what is known to different degrees of certainty ... Every one of the concepts of science is on a scale graduated somewhere between, but at neither end of, absolute truth and absolute falsity.'

you were talking about in the media, very quickly you found out you were actually talking about Jofra. Only once (I think) did I say something that was accidentally unguarded. Dean Wilson, the *Mirror*'s cricket correspondent, has a gift for asking exactly the right question, by which I mean getting you to give an answer that is more revealing than you'd intended. It was at the very end of a press conference, and I'd already said enough, but I took one more question, from Dean, who was sitting right next to me around the table at Lord's. 'How important, Ed, is experience in a massive tournament like the World Cup?'

'Experience takes many forms,' I replied.

He had his man. 'Definitely picking Jofra,' the correspondent said to himself, as he told me a few months later.

When you're sure

After the fact, when a selection goes well, it always becomes obvious. But if you return to the run-up to the spring of 2019, many people, including respected and informed voices, saw grounds for caution. Jonathan Agnew, the celebrated BBC commentator, described selecting Archer as a 'huge call'.

The day we announced the World Cup squad, an appropriately sunny spring day at Lord's, it felt the perfect fit for a group that was poised and ready. I cannot improve on the words Jonathan Liew published in the *Independent* the day after the squad was announced:

> And so, here we are: the 15 men who are widely held to have England's best chance of winning the World Cup in a generation. Seven play for counties in the South, six in the

> North, two in the Midlands. Eight were state-educated, seven privately educated. Three are from black or ethnic minority backgrounds, which roughly correlates to the UK population as a whole. They began life on four different continents, from Dublin to Cape Town, from Christchurch to Barbados ... Truly, these players are the best of us: a squad as rich and diverse as the islands they will be representing.

The World Cup campaign, as it turned out, would take England cricket to the edge of its seat and the limit of its nerves.

Personally, the day of the squad announcement brought home two reflections. First, it reminded me how much hidden work goes into a four-year cycle. England's journey had been shaped by many hands: Eoin Morgan, Andrew Strauss, coaches Trevor Bayliss and Paul Farbrace, and many others behind the scenes. For the last 13 months, relatively late in the story, I'd lived with the final pieces of the jigsaw constantly at the back of my mind.

Second, the announcement brought home that it's never too late to make a big decision. Yes, the World Cup plan had been in place for four years. And here was Jofra Archer, brought in just before midnight. But when you're sure, you're sure.

Two months later, watching the final in its glorious unpredictability, was a reminder of the unique nature of being a cricket selector: totally invested, but also detached from the furnace of competition. I watched the match from the ECB corporate box in the Grandstand at Lord's, side-on from the pitch, almost overhanging the edge of the outfield. The final boundary of England's batting Super Over landed maybe 25 yards to my left.

But a box at a cricket match, even one belonging to the governing body of the host nation and finalist, is still a kind of social event, and you're watching among people who are primarily there to enjoy the day.

James Taylor sat in the seat next to me almost the whole way through – excepting the odd bit of superstitious pacing around by one or the other of us. The seat on the other side was occupied by Sam Mendes, the theatre and film director, and we all swapped stories from sport and theatre. All performance is a shared stage; anyone who has lived it understands the intrinsic exposure to luck and circumstance, and the unique experience of watching your dreams play out, not only in public but also far beyond your control.

The narrative of the 2019 World Cup final, however tempting, does not need fully retelling here. The day began with rain, a delayed start, extended nerves, and shared tactical uncertainty about whether to bat or bowl first. Of the four possibilities (NZ win the toss and bowl, NZ win the toss and bat, England win the toss and bowl, England win the toss and bat), my favoured outcome was the one that happened: it was NZ's decision to make, and they opted to bat.

If you're interested in the influence of luck in sport, this final is the ultimate example. The arc of the match, in Simon Kuper's phrase in the *Financial Times*, 'practically summarised the book *Luck*'.

- Trent Boult accidentally steps on the boundary rope having pouched a skied catch: 'out' turns into 6 runs, and the match turns somersaults twice over inside one second.
- With England's chances slipping away again, a throw at the stumps deflects off Ben Stokes's bat, runs to the boundary for four over-throws – and 2 runs turns into 6.

No one has ever seen quite that sequence of events before. Few people at the time had a certain view on whether the correct verdict was 6 runs or 5 (as it should have been).

- Ben Stokes, player of the match, said he'd be apologising to Kane Williamson and New Zealand for 'the rest of his life'. Eoin Morgan, when I saw him after the match, said that the game was so rich in surprise and chance that it was 'hard to make sense of'.

It was the greatest and most unpredictable 50-over match of all time. In the late-evening sun, the stretched gold of high English summer that takes us back to the deep play of childhood nights, the match achieved an aesthetic as well as a sporting resolution. Cricket had scooped us up and held us all in magical thrall.

The criticism is occasionally made (especially in high artistic circles) that sport is a lower form of entertainment because there are only two basic plots: victory and defeat.* The World Cup final offered a convincing riposte. The story was textured, multi-layered and strangely complete – though not necessarily superficially 'fair'. Just like a great novel. My wife, a children's author, watching from the other side of the ground with the England players' families, said to me the next day that it was a richer experience than anything she'd known in the arts.

---

* During a debate on BBC Radio 3 in 2009 called 'Sport vs the Arts', this point was made by the Classical scholar Edith Hall: 'Sport has only two narratives, either you win or you lose – how boring.'

The wire

Before the Super Over, which would determine the World Cup, Jofra had already gone past every England bowler since the tournament was inaugurated in 1975: at the first time of asking, he'd taken more wickets (20) than any England bowler at any World Cup.

I had always assumed that Jofra, for all the other bowling talent on the field, was the man to bowl the Super Over. He is one of the best 'death' bowlers in the world, and he'd had a stellar tournament. But while it would be easy to make a statistical case that bowling Jofra was the 'right' decision, it was the way Eoin handled the personal situation which encapsulated England's World Cup project.

With the stakes so high, words – even very good words – are probably less important than presence. Eoin did what he so often does. He kept talking to the bowler, open in manner, conveying confidence, present and available – the very principles he'd outlined on that drive back from a selection meeting. The final scene, once again, revealed cool calculations interacting with the human touch.

I kept coming back to something Andrew Strauss – who had doubled down on Morgan's captaincy in 2015 and backed him to the hilt – had said to me 10 years earlier: 'It's not just about making the right decision. It's about making the decision right.' Yes, there is the position you've taken (which may have objective and scientific strands). Then there is also the art of bringing it to life in a human world – with persuasion, tact, management, leadership.

Morgan and Archer, chatting at the top of the bowler's mark with 1.6 billion people watching, encapsulated England's approach to the World Cup project. Analysis and rigour had lasered in on the right decision; accompanied by the equal understanding that there's always far more to it than that.

Archer is ready.

Flick, catch ...

Could be any moment ...

Flick, catch ...

Last ball, two to defend. Four years converge into one second. Archer gets another decision right, bowling tight to the batter, cramping Martin Guptill's swing of the bat – mishit to the outfield, Jason Roy's throw to the keeper's end, batter well short of safety, the bails are broken, England have won – 'by the barest of margins', in Ian Smith's great commentary, 'by the barest of margins'.

6
'Lego'

The concept of a swarm harmoniser really belongs to a wider principle: thinking in terms of teams rather than lists of individuals. When people asked me what a selector does, I would reply that a selector's job is to try 'to select winning teams'.

On one level this is factually incomplete, because selectors actually pick *squads* ranging from a 12-man squad for home Tests up to a 15- or 16-man squad for a tour overseas, from which the final XI is chosen by the captain/coach, in consultation with the selectors. But the essence of the answer is true. The point of selection (and recruitment more widely) is to maximise the output of the whole, not just to promote, employ or select 'deserving' individuals. This requires thinking about the team – its trajectory and confidence, the relations and interactions within it, and the subtle blend of its talents and capabilities. 'Choose the best player for every position,' argued Johan Cruyff, 'and you'll end up not with a strong XI, but with XI strong Is.' The way things fit together is at least as important as the pieces themselves.

Can you, then, identify the most appropriate players to solve the team's particular needs? 'I call him "Lego",' basketball GM Daryl Morey said about the undervalued performer Shane Battier. 'When he's on the court, all the pieces start to fit together.' Ironically, understanding this 'Lego' dimension is simultaneously getting harder and more important.

One of the problems with ultra-professionalism in sport, as in other spheres, is the trend towards extreme specialisation – and the resulting difficulties with seeing the wider picture. Sports teams, like businesses, increasingly chop themselves up into small sub-groups – attack coach, defence coach, transition coach, set-piece coach, kicking coach, and so on. Dedicated attention to small parts can have benefits, sometimes known as 'marginal gains'. But the specialisation trend also brings an opposite requirement: for someone who sees how the different pieces come together, and who can resist being unhelpfully influenced by specialists whose incentives might be skewed towards looking good personally (even if it's at the expense of the whole).

Looking at selection and recruitment in this way demands thinking about the wider context at least as much as about the individual player. Juanma Lillo, Pep Guardiola's mentor and now assistant manager at Manchester City, made the point well: 'My mentality is interaction and relation. If you say, "Let's evaluate the right back," I say, "But who is alongside him? Who is in front of him? Nearest to him?"' The right back could, superficially, appear to be playing badly. But was the real cause a failure of support from right midfield? Without understanding the context, it's very hard to evaluate performance fairly.

It is a commonplace in selecting rowing eights to accept that the final boat will not necessarily contain the 'best' eight rowers (in terms of quantitative aerobic capacity), because the race that matters is not the sum of eight separate solo efforts on a rowing machine in the gym, but instead a collective endeavour out on the water. The job of a coach and selector is to create the *fastest boat*.

A team can only be a living whole, and the whole is always different from the sum of its parts. That is true even in sports which superficially appear to be a series of independent events, such as cricket and baseball, as well as sports which have intrinsic movement flow, such as football, or a single collective pull, such as rowing.

It is a myth, as the cliché has it, that cricket is 'a team game played by individuals'. It is, in fact, an individual game played by teams. You need 'Lego' players in cricket, too. And in most professions.

'Lego' players

We recalled the 25-year-old opening batter Keaton Jennings to the England Test team during the 2018 series versus Pakistan. Like many of his peers, Jennings had a Test average in the mid-20s, and had been dropped from the side 12 months previously. Over the next 11 games, Jennings maintained almost exactly the same average, 25 overall.

Given this return in terms of cold average runs per completed innings, some observers argued that Jennings was given 'too long a run' in the side by the selectors. He was routinely described as a 'favourite', which of course was meant as a dig at us, not the player. It is certainly true that his sequence of games in the team was almost twice as long as he'd been given first time around (six games), despite similar returns. That was quite typical for our selection era: we were prepared to resist external pressure to drop players.

Should we have dropped Jennings sooner? That case was often made. After a disappointing final match in the 2018 series versus India, and an overall average of 19 for that summer, many predicted Jennings would be deselected from the England Test tour to Sri Lanka that winter.

That wasn't the case: Jennings was selected in the squad to face Sri Lanka. There were three reasons. First, it had been an especially hard summer for everyone in the opening batting position – 20 was the median average for openers going into the final Test, pretty much exactly Jennings's record. Second, Jennings had proven ability in the exact conditions that we were about to encounter next – against spin in Asia, where he'd made an accomplished hundred on Test debut two years before. Third, Jennings had the personality to endure difficult challenges in his own performances while still contributing positively to the mood and outlook of the whole team. Watching him carefully in the team environment, it was clear that even when things were very tough for him as an individual, he did not retreat as a person or an influence. In short, he was bringing real character to an extremely difficult role.

Those three factors were all central in approaching selection: first, context; second, suitability for conditions; third, the team dimension.

And just when the personal pressure was greatest, following the difficult India series, Jennings responded with the performance of his life: 146 not out in a superb 1st Test win against Sri Lanka in their stronghold at Galle. That evening in the team hotel, finishing a round of television interviews in front of the

Indian Ocean, he remained, in success, exactly the same balanced and consistent human being – happy, certainly, but still very much the same man who'd had to battle through a tough series against India a few weeks earlier.

That characteristic – equability and constancy amid an intense and public challenge – was one of the things that made Jennings a net positive on the team overall. Jennings played 11 Test matches during my spell as selector, many of them under personal pressure about his place in the team. England won nine of those 11 games.

Obviously, there are limits to how much we can infer from 11 games. First, the sample size is small from a statistical perspective. But that is a function of analysing performance in a format in which each game lasts for five days. Eleven matches constitutes nearly a *full year* of Test matches (which numbered 14 Tests in that cycle) – quite a contrast from 162 stat-rich games in a Major League Baseball season.

Further, despite the team's excellent performance over the previous 11 games, Jennings did end up being dropped – by the selection panel that I led. Why? As always, we were assessing player confidence, and whether he needed to find some new technical solutions to the questions being set by world-class bowlers. We came to the view that if Keaton could improve in one or two areas, he could come back again as a more complete player.

Jennings was replaced by Joe Denly, who shared some similar qualities in terms of character and taking on difficult roles for the good of the team (while averaging 30 to Jennings's 25). Denly's time in the team also included the toughest technical challenge of the lot, playing five Tests against a superb Australian bowling attack in 2019.

So the principle endured, even though the players changed. In filling an extremely demanding and often thankless role, the team needed a player with the emotional and psychological resilience to continue facing up to personal challenges with little fuss and absolutely no self-pity. Of all the Test players England selected in this period, Jennings and Denly were among the most underrated.

I wouldn't expect either player to agree with our decision to drop them from the team in the end. But I would be disappointed if the two players did not feel that the selectors strongly supported them all the way through and, above all, valued them. And they can know for sure that they contributed to a winning England team.

Opposite and not

At first glance, Yorkshire wrist-spinner Adil Rashid would seem to belong to a very different category. Where Jennings is a resilient Stoic, Rashid is a dazzling entertainer – multi-talented, skilful, capable of changing any match with a flick of the wrist. And yet in terms of overall effect, they both contributed to a team which was more than the sum of its parts.

Before I joined the selection group, Rashid had been left out of the Test team for the previous 18 months while becoming increasingly irreplaceable in England's ODI and T20 teams. His confidence, mastery and centrality to English cricket were becoming more obvious every month.

With Rashid in superb white-ball form, and injury and county selection limiting game-time opportunities for alternative spinners Jack Leach and Dom Bess, I kept asking myself the same question: 'Would the opposition rather see Rashid selected in Tests for England or continuing to be left out?' And the answer would surely have been that they'd be more comfortable knowing Rashid was *not* on the pitch. It's a decent rule of thumb: do what the opposition least wants you to do.

For that reason, I was always slightly baffled that our selection of Rashid – who had not been playing red-ball cricket for Yorkshire for a while – attracted so much controversy. (As just one example, the *Daily Telegraph* led with the headline: 'Rashid selection a stab in the back for county cricket'.)

Ideally, clearly, all England Test players would play four-day cricket for their counties (on the rare occasions when England's multi-format players were available for county selection). But it seemed odd that this brilliant all-round cricketer, who brought so much sparkle and talent to England's teams, was being singled out for criticism.

In fact, the motivation to bring him back had been very simple: the selectors all felt England was a stronger Test squad with Rashid in it, and I was happy to front a decision – however controversial – that we all believed would be good for the team.

In the immediate term, however, Adil found himself at the centre of a selection controversy. And I felt deeply responsible. The day before the 1st Test against India – which Sam Curran would swing England's way – I met up with Adil in a coffee shop close to the England team hotel in Birmingham. I wanted him to leave our informal chat feeling that he could focus on simply enjoying the match and expressing his talent and skill. And that we would back him to the hilt.

The next morning – day one of the series and the opening chapter of Adil's Test comeback – I got to the ground unusually early, soaking up every drop of atmosphere and tension there. By chance, that gave me the opportunity to watch a perceptive piece of coaching. From about 10.30 a.m. to 10.45 a.m., with the crowd swelling and the minutes counting down towards first ball, England's spin coach Saqlain Mushtaq (a wonderful bowler for Pakistan and Surrey) sat cross-legged on the outfield, just in front of the stands, with Adil – the two men chatting, laughing and talking through their shared art. My reading of events was that Saqlain wanted to be present alongside Adil in the moments before the match, sharing every possible last step, before the curtain was raised for good. I felt very much the same way.

The match ended up being dominated by faster bowlers, not spinners. But Adil chipped in throughout, especially at the denouement. On the final day, with India needing just 43 to win and 2 wickets remaining, Rashid trapped Ishant Sharma LBW – only for the on-field umpire to give it not out. When the decision was overturned on TV review I celebrated more raucously – happily, off-camera – than you'd expect of a man in a sober suit and tie. Moments later, England had won a classic Test.

There was another supportive presence in the background that week at Edgbaston, and it was a player vying for the same spot in the team that had gone to Adil: the off-spinner and all-rounder Moeen Ali. Moeen and Adil (stalwarts of the ODI and T20 teams) are great friends, and Moeen always encouraged Adil's return to Test cricket, even if, as for this Test match, it came at the expense of his own place in the team. Moeen is one of the most unselfish cricketers, and throughout that summer I'd see Adil and Moeen working together and supporting each other at net practice.

Five months later, the two men both contributed superbly in the series against Sri Lanka, where England were led off the field in the final Test by Rashid, having taken a match-winning

5–49, the culmination of an underestimated series of personal contributions with both bat and ball. Most importantly, it was our seventh Test win in eight matches.

Sadly, after only one more Test, a recurrent shoulder injury – that niggled away during the World Cup year in 2019 – led Adil to step back from Test cricket and focus on ODIs and T20s, where workload and wear and tear are far lower. While he remains one of England's most irreplaceable players in the shorter formats, his absence has been a significant blow to the Test team's ability to win matches in all conditions.

Along with Sam Curran, Jennings and Rashid had the best win–loss percentages of all England Test players during the three years under review. They all helped us build better team performance.

What do the three players have in common? On one level, almost nothing. They do not belong to a particular 'type' of player, beyond the fact that they added to the collective output. All three players possessed qualities that England needed at the time. They made the team better, just by being themselves.

In searching for 'Lego players' – in sport or any high-performance team – you're not looking at individual attributes in isolation. It's always about seeing how one last addition can improve the overall puzzle. And there's no point searching for the piece before you understand what's missing.

'Lego' models

The conventional template for a Test team is five batters, one all-rounder at number six, wicketkeeper at seven, then four specialist bowlers.

And yet the most successful Test teams typically set up in the way that suits the talent they possess, even if that means diverging from the conventional template:

- For the Australian 'Invincibles' of 1948, the all-rounder Keith Miller batted at four (unusually high for an all-rounder) and opened the bowling.
- In the unrivalled West Indies team of the 1980s, they mostly declined to play any all-rounders or spinners – batters from one to six, then the wicketkeeper, then four fearsome quicks.
- In the world-leading Australian team of the late 1990s and 2000s, they usually (though not always) selected just four bowlers and no designated all-rounder – three quicks and the greatest spinner of all, Shane Warne.

It's not being 'conventional' that helps a team to win. It's maximising what you've got.

It is extremely unconventional, for example, to select six bowlers for a Test match. As we've just discussed, some of the greatest teams picked only four. But during my three years involved with selection, England selected six recognised bowlers for nine matches – winning seven, losing none and drawing two.

In this six-bowler team structure, the central all-rounder Ben Stokes, who commands a place as a batter anyway, was not required to bowl too much. Stokes's bowling was a very handy bonus rather than an expectation; sometimes it was called on, sometimes it wasn't.

Here is the fascinating thing. England had full 'volition' over playing six bowlers on only two occasions. On the other seven occasions, Stokes was carrying an injury, and couldn't guarantee bowling a full allocation of overs, so we dropped a specialist batter and selected an extra all-rounder instead.

Every single one of these games when team formation was at least partly 'forced' – including the draws (which would both have been wins if not for the weather) – the team's performance was excellent:

- 4th Test vs India, 2018, won by 60 runs, sealing the series win
- 5th Test vs India, 2018, won by 118 runs, extending the series win to 4–1
- 5th Test vs Australia, 2019, won by 135 runs, levelling the series 2–2
- 3rd Test vs West Indies, 2020, won by 269, sealing the series 2–1
- 1st Test vs Pakistan, 2020, won by 3 wickets, drawing ahead 1–0
- 2nd Test vs Pakistan, 2020, rain-affected drawn
- 3rd Test vs Pakistan, 2020, rain-affected drawn

There were a number of advantages, given England's talent distribution, for the six-bowler structure. It reduced the physical strain and workload on a champion cricketer (Stokes). Six bowlers also maximised England's talent on the field, bringing an extra cricketer of real quality (Curran, Woakes or Moeen) into a more central role in the team. And it usually moved Buttler to number six, where he averages 47 in Tests.

There are two wider observations here and, following on from them, one difficult question.

First, with England's Test performances over recent years, the most successful periods have coincided with team formation being *more* surprising. The more the conventional team selection, the *less* England win. Second, when England's hand was forced and we were pushed into the brave position of playing one fewer batters, team performance was always impressive. These circumstances made us flexible and adaptable, which were exactly our strengths anyway: with more all-round talents in the team, there is greater fluidity in the roles they can perform.

Now for the more difficult part. Why did it take circumstances beyond our control to make us arrive at a team structure that worked so well? We could have chosen to do it all the time. We could have played the extra all-rounder in place of a specialist batter, even when Stokes was completely fit.

We did exactly that in just one series, choosing to set up with that audacious six-bowler structure at the outset – in Sri Lanka in 2018. That series ended with England's Test team reaching its highest world ranking, number two, since 2012. We should have persevered with it.

This is the debate that I most regret failing to win more often – not about individual players, but about team formation.

There is nothing inherently or permanently superior about six bowlers rather than five (or even four). For England in this spell, however, increasing the number of all-rounders generally brought our strengths centre-stage and reduced the areas where we were comparatively weak.

It's far from a cure-all solution. In a different context – including, potentially, England's Test team in future years – five or four bowlers might turn out to be a better fit than six. But from 2019–21, and this is just a personal view, I think we were too easily knocked off the winning formula of summer and autumn 2018.

I blame myself for not making the case more effectively.

Systems

Orientating selection and recruitment around the team's needs can inevitably lead to talented or famous players missing out – with all the potential for the noise and disgruntlement that follows. Sir Alf Ramsey left out his superstar striker Jimmy Greaves – and won the 1966 World Cup. Warren Gatland dropped British and Irish Lions legend Brian O'Driscoll for the decider against Australia in 2013 – creating a huge backlash against Gatland, but also bringing about an excellent performance and a series win.

The problems come when leaders *stop* making difficult selection decisions that serve the team, because in doing so they are turning away from the most important lever under their control.

Figuring out what the team requires, however, is usually a complex, subtle question that demands weighing and integrating many different kinds of information. It is also a never-ending imaginative exercise: because the team is always developing, its needs change constantly.* The best decision-makers discern what's needed quicker and then move more decisively. That's why Manchester United under Sir Alex Ferguson never required a dedicated 'rebuilding phase'. The team was being renewed constantly. He thought not only *about teams*; he thought *in teams*.

---

* 'Organisations ... should be viewed as their individual members are: as a living thing whose collective instincts evolve in the fight for advantage,' Matthew Parris has argued. The same applies to teams. Good leaders can steer those instincts.

Russell Ackoff, the American systems thinker, asked his students to imagine a lecture hall filled with the best component parts drawn from every car manufacturer (the best brakes, the best suspension and so on). If all the best bits were then assembled, would it create the best single car? Of course not, Ackoff argued, because 'the automobile is the product of the interaction of the parts, not the sum of the parts taken separately'. The *way* a car fits together, to a significant degree, constitutes the majority of what a car manufacturer does.

> This has an incredibly important implication for management which the Western world has not yet learnt ... If it's a corporation, you divide into production, marketing, finance, personnel and so on; if it's a university, you break up into departments, curricula, programmes – and then try to manage each one on the assumption that when this is done the whole will run as well as possible. That's absolutely false ... It's the way the parts fit together that determines the system not how they perform taken separately.

The car component fallacy applies even more strongly to teams. The way parts fit together into the whole not only influences collective output but also influences the measured output of each individual: if you can create a superior whole, then the individuals suddenly look a lot better, even if they are considered individually.

This concept has been taken one step further by the neuroscientist Iain McGilchrist (author of *The Master and His Emissary* (2009) and *The Matter with Things* (2021)). In any complex situation, thinking about isolated and separate 'parts' misses out what matters most. The team shapes the individuals as much as the individuals shape the team. 'Relationships are primary, more foundational than the things related,' McGilchrist argues, 'relationships don't just "connect" pre-existing things, but modify what we mean by the "things".' In this context, McGilchrist is not using 'relationships' to mean 'how people get along with one another socially'. He means 'how they relate to each other fundamentally in the creation of the whole'.

Put differently, 'team-building' – far from being a slippery concept implying cushy off-site days at the go-karting circuit – is actually the *core activity* of anyone whose job it is to create a high-performing team, in sport or business.

Selection, like recruiting talent more widely, is only partly about evaluating the merits of two or more individuals vying for one place in the team. There is a preceding question, usually more difficult and more important: what are the needs of the team and how will individuals interact in shaping the whole collective?

It's a misread to think of 'team-building' as a secondary or fluffy idea; it is primary and fundamental.

7
Sources of Confidence

When I was a young professional cricketer, I used to watch a VHS videotape of the legendary 1974 fight between Muhammad Ali and George Foreman again and again (it is featured in the classic boxing documentary *Champions Forever*.) A few seconds of the fight, at the very end of the third round, captivated me, perhaps obsessed me.

By the end of the third, Ali has established the pattern of the fight: long spells lying deep on the ropes, absorbing wild body punches from Foreman, as Ali bewilders and tires out the stronger, younger fighter. In several rounds, as the closing seconds approach, Ali springs into life and stings Foreman with slick combinations of punches. After taunting the bull into over-confidence, the matador applies his treatment.

The end of the third, however, is a case apart, even within the pattern of late-Ali counter-attacks. The two sets of combinations, seven blows within eight seconds, is the best boxing of the fight.

This time, as the bell sounds, Ali has to be peeled off Foreman by the referee (for much of the fight it is the other way around, with Ali clinging on cagily). Not now. Ali's blood is up. And the fleeting clash is over too quickly for his tastes. Ali stalks around Foreman on the way to his corner, askance superiority mixed with something more visceral. He has, in those lethal and joyful few seconds, let his own guard down. It doesn't seem like a strategy, or a mind-game – not this time. In that instant, as he is being pushed to his corner, Ali looks to be on the point of near-madness – an inspired kind of madness. Ali is momentarily out of control, within a wider pattern of total control – a kind of higher confidence, beyond mere tactics.

Ali being Ali, he's talking and taunting throughout much of this. But the voice that matters here isn't really about the words he speaks, but his voice as an athlete. He has total trust in himself to judge when to move in and out of control, without planning quite how or when. Ali doesn't know what he's doing, while also knowing exactly what he's doing.

I thought back to that classic round of boxing during the most remarkable cricket innings any of us had ever seen, at Headingley in 2019. Ben Stokes, during his unbeaten 135 vs Australia, moved between calculated manipulation of the strike (the deft dink and a scampered single) and then brutal, primal swings of the bat for six, *all within a few seconds*.

The whole man played that innings. Within each over of six balls (roughly five minutes of play), Stokes was accessing every corner of his competitive talent, from the coolest thinking to extreme risk-taking exuberance. Whatever astonishing risk he'd just pulled off, Stokes was immediately able to reset, and find calmness and control once again – just as Muhammad Ali, though he enjoyed his alpha showdown at the end of the third round, surrounded it with technical restraint and poise.

Masters of Go

In autumn 2012, I watched Roger Federer and Novak Djokovic contest the ATP World final in London. At the time, they were ranked No. 1 and No. 2 in the world. Federer won the first two games to love, and won the third as well. In total, he'd won 10 of the first 12 points, with winners landing perfectly on the line. (Rafael Nadal describes these phases of Federer play as like 'being in a hurricane'. All you can do is hope that when it passes you've been able to survive.)

Federer likes to start quickly, to dominate, establish the pattern of benign dictatorship. When he needs to, he can be a great defensive player, too, but it's only ever a means to an end. He defends in order to attack again, to get things back on to his terms. I have never seen Federer win a match as the more defensively orientated player.

Gradually, over the course of the first set (which began 3–0 Federer after 12 points), something strange happened. Federer continued to hit the ball as cleanly as ever. But Djokovic started to retrieve apparently impossible positions, time and time again. The hard-court slide, which Djokovic pioneered, allowed him not only to reach further but to move back into position quicker. Slide, retrieve, balance, sprint, slide, retrieve, balance – on repeat, over and over. It was like watching a highlights reel of Michael Hooper playing number seven in rugby: quick to the tackle, even quicker back on his feet, over the tackled player, penalty to Australia ...

No sooner had you finished admiring Federer's latest 'winner' than you realised it wasn't a winner after all, it was back in play and the point was alive. Federer continued to hit 'winner' after 'winner', only they were being turned into routine rallying shots.

Djokovic's defensive movement was so complete that no corner of the baseline was safe from his gliding feet and elastic limbs. The court was being sealed off, brick by brick. And Federer's beautiful attacking shots were crashing into a solid wall.

In the process, both sides of the equation changed. Djokovic's defensive confidence deepened, and Federer's offensive confidence weakened. That Federer was hitting the ball so well compounded the problem. He was both executing brilliantly and also falling short – a troubling tactical situation.

Both men played in their own style, their preferred manner, and superbly. That made it a complete form of competitive conversation. Federer used his voice – 'I attack, I strike the ball more sweetly, I don't back down' – knowing that when he plays that well, he wins, almost always. And Djokovic had his answer ready: 'Not against me. And not today.'

In 1938 the novelist Yasunari Kawabata wrote a set of newspaper reports on a series of Go matches, the Oriental board game, between the two leading players.

Sushai, the 'invincible Master', is presented as an ageing representative of Japan's courtly traditions. Otake, the younger and more forceful rival, emerges as his rational and scientific counterpoint. During the draining eight-month contest, it becomes clear that the fading Master will lose not only the match but also his life. This final match is the Master's last stand. After the war, Kawabata revisited and revised his match reports, publishing them as a novel, *The Master of Go* (1951).

As the match progresses, two types of competitor are revealed, driven by opposite temperaments. So the novel becomes a study of psychological contrast. We discover their differing voices as players.

The Master sought inspiration. In contrast, Otake, unable or unwilling to 'lose himself', is driven by the fear of losing. The Master, with disdain for trivia, 'would indifferently play his stones with either side up'. Otake is obsessive about irrelevant details – if one of the stones is played upside down, he has to readjust it. Otake is noisy and assertive during matches. The Master exuded a quietness 'that cooled and cleaned the air around him'.

Though we know where the novelist's loyalties lie – observing the Master enter the contest, Kawabata wonders if he is witnessing a Zen 'passage to enlightenment' – he has a reporter's sense of fairness.

So the novel, like watching a great sports match, expands our understanding of how high achievement derives from a broad range of psychological types. Though the narrator cannot hide his instincts, that doesn't prevent his story from demonstrating that there are many approaches to mastery. Between the lines, we see how competitive diversity accidentally helps to make games so civilising and surprising: there can never be a single path to greatness. What the two players share, perhaps only this, is that they have learnt their own way, finding confidence in their own particular voice.

Undivided self

Voice is where sport and literature overlap creatively. Both the writer and the athlete – even if the latter doesn't use the term – know they are in deep trouble if they lose their voice. No surprise, then, that it's in this domain that the writer tracks the athlete with closest familiarity, trying to recognise and interpret in others what he knows is central in his own life. Fascination with voice, the mysterious process by which character and feeling turn into expression and output, is what entranced me during that O2 final, what turned that boxing third round into an obsession, and why I couldn't put down Kawabata's *The Master of Go.*

In *The Master and His Emissary*, Iain McGilchrist explores the interaction of the two halves of the brain. The Left Hemisphere, though it excels at laser-beam focus, is prone to overconfidence and outbursts of frustrated anger. The Right Hemisphere sees the whole and how we relate to it. So McGilchrist stresses the importance of *co-operation* between the Left and Right Hemispheres – the balance and union, if you like, of your often divided self.

McGilchrist doesn't apply his theory to sportsmen and women. But I think the kind of co-operation he describes is at play in athletes when they are operating at their supreme psychological range, as they move quickly and intuitively between apparently contradictory styles and modes.

As a cricket selector, the players I most believed in had reached an accommodation with their full character. As shorthand we might say, 'they knew who they were', though that wouldn't be quite accurate. It's not so much about knowing themselves as *being* themselves. In contrast, I often felt a wariness about players I thought had a 'mixed method' (psychologically). These players set up their performance methodology in unhappy opposition with their deeper instincts. In effect, how they *thought they wanted to play* was in conflict with *how they needed to play*. Under pressure, they didn't know which version of themselves to back or which one to trust.

In contrast, the best players are able to direct their actions and decisions in a way that corresponds with the source of their deepest confidence. They make good decisions, in other words, by being in step with themselves. That's also why the most authentic players find the game less intrinsically stressful: when you're being yourself, you take less out of yourself. (Here professional sport mirrors what we all know to be true in an informal setting: social life without authenticity becomes an exhausting performance.)

'It's just not fair'

Carlo Ancelotti, the urbane and decorated football manager, tells a story about when he was a young player at Roma, under the direction of the Swedish manager Nils Liedholm. After a night out on the town, Ancelotti and two teammates drove back to the team hotel with two women in the back seat. Liedholm strode towards the car and the players braced themselves for a dressing down from their manager. Instead, Liedholm peered inside the car window; 'Is there any room for me?' he asked.

Instead of cementing the separation between two generations, Liedholm had given them all a story to share – a light touch and a memorable moment. The coach had also subtly shown that he had an answer for every situation. That kind of wit and mischief, Ancelotti realised, would be tools he'd use himself when it was his turn to be a manager.

In lesser hands, the same response wouldn't have been memorable and effective, but plain soft – a walkover manager. Which is another way of saying that the critical factor is not what was said, but the voice behind it. (My father, a teacher and writer, refers to 'voice' as the 'invisible ink' in communication.)

When I was 23, I batted in partnership with future England opener Rob Key for hours against an extremely unthreatening part-time spin bowler in a first-class match. When Rob and I got back to the dressing room – undefeated and with 50s to our names – we were greeted by the ex-captain and teacher John Inverarity, who had just joined Kent as head coach.

'They tell me you can both play a bit,' Inverarity began, in his clipped Australian accent, 'and that you want to get selected as batters in the England team. For argument's sake, let's say you're both a seven out of ten. Maybe six and a half. Well, the bloke out there bowling at you is a two. And do you know how you've responded? You're batting as though you are both hovering around the two out of ten level yourselves. You've gone down to his level rather than demanding he comes up to yours. Now get out there and play! Use your feet, hit the ball, expand your game.' *Six and a half out of ten? Gone down to two out of ten?* This was a new kind of discourse with management.

And yet two cocky young players – who rarely shied away from argument – looked at each other with big smiles. By criticising us with such a wry and amused tone, and so bluntly, the coach had, of course, paid us a great compliment. He believed we were better than we yet believed. Inverarity had shown us that he wanted us to be more ambitious – and he wasn't going to let us off the hook. From that moment, our form as batters radically improved, and we both had breakthrough seasons. Rob was playing for England within a year. Inverarity's manifest confidence in his own judgement inspired confidence in our own batting.

In his radio programme *The Art of Directing*, the England cricket captain Mike Brearley asked how effective leaders exert a creative impact on groups. Brearley's guest, the theatre director Peter Hall, argued that double injustice is at play: the greater the creative talent of the director, the more their advice takes on its own aura of effectiveness. Hall reflected that he'd observed bad directors give brilliant advice – with poor results. And he'd heard good directors give awful advice – with brilliant results. It just wasn't fair.

Against the myth of 'management techniques' which claim that leadership skills can be learnt from scratch (like buying flat-pack furniture), impact in real life tends to be determined by insight and authenticity – by confidence and voice.

Using the same logic, I don't believe that effective decision-making can be learnt *solely theoretically*. Instead, in reading this book, I hope some readers will feel greater confidence about carrying out decisions *which they already sensed were right* – as I have been emboldened by the decision-makers I've observed and studied.

'Not you'

Early in my time as selector, there was a last-minute injury replacement required. The player was unlikely to play in the final XI, but he was needed in the squad in case there were injuries or tactical changes before the game.

This latest decision came soon after an extended series of big calls, some of them controversial. My first instinct this time was to play it safe, a kind of risk-averse 'status quo selection'. When I talked things through with my close colleagues, they saw things differently. One of them put it like this: 'You may be right that it won't affect events on the field anyway, but you've always said: "Every selection is an opportunity." That's how you like to approach decisions. This decision is an opportunity, too.'

There was a blunter version, left between the lines: 'Play it safe, miss an opportunity? That's not who you are.' Effective decision-making should not only be principled and unbiased, it also has a voice, a tilt, a spirit.

The most reliable gauge of our deepest confidence is the truthfulness of our voice. I had (momentarily, I hope) lost mine. It was typically good advice from very strong colleagues to nudge me back on track. We changed tack, and selected for the first time the exciting Sussex batter Phil Salt.

8
Policy?

In 1984, Alexander Chancellor wrote a farewell notebook in the *Spectator*, which he was leaving:

> When I joined the paper as editor in 1975, people were in the habit of asking me what my 'policy' was going to be ... How desperately uneasy the question made me. If there was a lavatory in the vicinity, I would lock myself inside it. I was sure I ought to have a 'policy' ... but I most certainly hadn't got one.

His deputy editor, Charles Moore, said that Chancellor, when pressed on his 'editorial policy' by bosses or big advertisers, would reply: 'Well, we should publish some good articles, I suppose.'

Here was an editor at the top of his profession, shrugging off a probing question about his editorial philosophy with the answer that it was better to have good articles in a magazine rather than bad ones. Moore added that Chancellor was genuinely troubled by not having a high-concept soundbite about 'policy'. Instead, just 'some good articles'. What kind of policy or philosophy is that?

But consider the superb advantages of 'we should publish some good articles', and how a more prescriptive answer would have been a hostage to fortune. Beneath Chancellor's self-deprecation and charm there was also shrewdness and self-confidence. He didn't need a policy because he backed his judgement.

I often remembered Chancellor's deft reply when people asked me the equivalent question: 'What kind of player are you looking to select for England?' The Chancellor line, 'Oh, we should pick some good players,' is a far better answer than most.

Because whatever selection policy you describe in theory, there will always come the day when you undermine it in practice. In fact, any prescriptive answer you give to the question 'What kind of player are you looking for?' is unlikely to survive much scrutiny – or survive for long – even if you start out with the best intentions.

'We are looking for players who demand selection through consistently high performances at the level below England, in county cricket ...' Well, unfortunately, that policy would rule out selecting on potential, which was the basis for some of the most celebrated call-ups in England's history (such as Duncan Fletcher's selection of Marcus Trescothick in 2000, who became a superb England player despite a moderate record at county level). On the flip side, nor would you want to be honour-bound to pick a high-performing county player, if everyone agreed that his game was clearly unsuited to international cricket.

OK then, couldn't *the reverse* be the policy? 'We are looking for players with the potential to be great England players ...'

Unfortunately, that policy would rule out the counterpoint: selecting a competent player who will do a decent job in the absence of a brilliant alternative, providing immediate ballast in the team today, while also potentially providing more time for a truly top-flight player to develop in the wings.

So it's tough to come down on one side or the other in the 'potential versus performance' axis. But surely there has to be a pathway into the England team? How about selecting on England 'Lions' form?

Hmm, sounds good in theory. But the England Lions have a very irregular schedule. For example, 21 months passed between February 2020 and November 2021 without a single Lions match being played (Covid was part of this, of course). Further, it's not uncommon for next-in-line England players to step back, even if selected, from a Lions tour so they can either play franchise cricket (as Liam Livingstone has done at the IPL or the Australian T20 Big Bash) or to get a break from a busy few years on the road and recharge (as Ben Foakes has done). While it's attractive to have a 'pathway', do you really want to eliminate the possibility of selecting players such as Foakes and Livingstone for England because they've missed Lions cricket?

'Specialists, we need to pick specialists – that's a policy ...' This popular refrain has two dimensions. First, it can mean 'specialists in that format' (that is, a Test 'specialist' would be a new player who wasn't already playing for England in a different format, such as T20). Second, specialist can mean 'specialist for a particular position' – such as a specialist opening batter, or a specialist number three. Neither category of 'specialist', unfortunately for its advocates, has turned out to be a reliable gauge of high performance in an England shirt.

Indeed, most of the players who've been selected and dropped from the Test team over the last five years were very much red-ball specialists (Westley, Hameed, Sibley and so on). And many of them played in their specialist position (Westley at three, as he does for Essex, the others as openers, as they do for their counties).

Let's flip that concept, too, then: 'Give us proven winners, and let's back them to adapt in new circumstances!' This was the logic that led many people, including the selectors, to advocate Jason Roy, fresh from guiding England to the ODI World Cup in 2019, being added to the Test matches that immediately followed. But Roy was dropped from the Test team after that summer amid considerable rewriting of history among pundits. For the record, though Jason didn't succeed as he would have hoped in the limited opportunities he was given – bloody selectors! – I do not think the original decision was irrational. And I don't think it should close down the cross-format route into the England team in the future.

Any approach to selection demands agility, which in turn demands shrewd communication (addressed at the end of this chapter). It might feel tempting, when pressed by a player or journalist, to dress up a judgement as a hard-and-fast rule. Tempting in the short term, but risky over the long term. Because reasons change as the context changes. And strict consistency for consistency's sake is an impediment to getting the right answer; you can become a prisoner of policy. 'He does not care what he says, so long as it is true,' the philosopher R. G. Collingwood wrote admiringly of a colleague. 'In this freedom from anxiety lies the secret of his success.'

As teasing out different 'policies' reveals, I don't think selectors should close down *any* routes into the England team.

Instead, the selectors should assess all the differing kinds of evidence, for all different kinds of player, and make a balanced overall judgement that best serves the England team.

And that conclusion, in fact, takes Chancellor's logic to the next level. Not just 'some good pieces'; but some good pieces *that improve the overall magazine*. Not just some good players, but some good players who will *improve the England team*.

I'd make one exception to scepticism about policy or types of player. If there is a 'type' that selectors should tilt towards, it is not a category or a descriptor – 'specialist', 'Lions player', 'county performer' – but a characteristic.

Machiavelli termed it *virtù*. *Virtù* was about character, but in particular the application of character in the acquisition of worldly success: character not just as an end in itself, but character powering achievement. For a person of *virtù*, in other words, inner qualities are bound up with outward achievement. In short: success. That, I think, is the 'type' of player that selectors should look for: players whose temperament is innately bound up with the need to achieve; players who enhance the performance, the authority and the standing of the team.

Can the team itself – not just individuals within it – develop *virtù* of its own? That's the ultimate challenge. It's also a definition of institutional wisdom, when the team's character imperceptibly improves the behaviour of everyone inside it.

Family? Business? Neither?

Sports organisations – even national governing bodies – often talk to the public as a FTSE 100 company might address potential shareholders. The language of sport reflects this pivot:

phrases like 'stakeholders' and 'partners' are now commonplace (and 'pivot', for that matter). But a national sport is not building up to a flotation, it is bound up with the fabric and identity of the nation. In this context, being clear about your purpose isn't just a question of wordplay.

Every organisation has to know the kind of activity at its core. 'What are we about?' is the question that outranks all the others. So you may have noticed a revealing contradiction in the language of modern sport. On the one hand, sport increasingly uses rhetoric from big business. And yet, amid this corporatisation, sports teams also refer to themselves as having the characteristics of a family. A family club. A real family atmosphere. We're one family. Like a family.

This cosy terminology is designed to emphasise the non-transactional dimensions of life inside elite sport: togetherness, shared experience, lasting bonds.

Both metaphors – whether aping a FTSE 100 company or pretending to be a nuclear family – derive from a misplaced sense of insecurity. The aspiration towards business springs from the perception that sport is still too emotional and amateurish. The claim to be one big family protects against the opposite anxiety: that sport is uncomfortably brutal and Darwinian.

The language of family could be used across many settings: an orchestra, the cast of a play, a circus, a dance company. Anyone who has been part of a journey towards improved collective performance, at any level, will know how intimacy and the feeling of great connection accompanies the sense of shared mission. Sport is just one example.

But does emotional closeness really equate to a family? Surely not.

A professional sports team directly links income with performance: it pays more money to people who are perceived to be the higher achievers. You'd be concerned about any family which siphoned off more pocket money to the child with higher exam grades.

A sports team is compelled to deselect players, often permanently and without prior consultation. Where there is a transfer market, the player is sold. Where there isn't a transfer market, the player is simply 'cut' (in American parlance). Aside from Thomas Hardy novels or tragic situations, families do not trade their own children in the marketplace.

Any player entering a professional sports team knows that although the achievement is permanent – they have represented an elite team – their *current status* as a selected player is temporary and provisional. Very temporary and very provisional. In contrast, a family (nearly always) wants membership to be permanent and not subject to conditions.

A sports team has a moral obligation to move beyond players – however great they have been in the past – who no longer command selection. When loyalty to past achievement trumps current merit, the team and its fans are deprived of what they both deserve. There shouldn't be a place for sentimentality.

In short, I wouldn't want to belong to any family that functioned like an elite sports team. That is not a criticism of sports teams but an acceptance of their intrinsic differences. A family which demonstrated a sports team's never-ending and unsentimental focus on performance would be terrifying to observe, let alone live inside. Elite sport is not like any family I want to belong to and it doesn't benefit by pretending it is.

Michael Atherton, on presenting Ben Duckett with his England cap in 2016, perfectly summarised the sense of an unbroken tradition. 'The wonderful thing about owning one of these,' Atherton said to Duckett, 'is that you are immediately part of something that is bigger, better and more meaningful than yourself; it provides a link right back to 1877 to the many players that came before you and provides a link to the many hundreds who will come after you.' That is apt, and a reminder that the concept applies in many domains. It doesn't have to be a 'family'. You are joining a club, an enterprise, a collective.

In the case of England cricket, how might we capture this peculiar quality?

It has a textured history and a rich stock of shared memories.

It has great champions who've galvanised the team and inspired the nation.

It's been served by many different kinds of ambition, open to various routes to the top.

It has its legends and folklore, half-truths and exaggerations.

It indulges inconsistencies and contradictions as well as shared truths.

It has cartoonish enemies, who are often really much-needed allies in our trade.

It has inevitably suffered passing humiliations and periods of retrenchment.

It has endured, and remembers fondly those who add to its glory.

It is, in other words, a kind of city state – with its great battle heroes, shrewd officers and unforgettable artists. And, like any great city state, its reputation is always in flux. It is always revisiting old truths, revising its narratives, always hoping for more in the future. You need to know its past in order to shape its future.

A FTSE company? I don't think so. 'Our' business (if we must use the term) is creating memories, bringing glory and inspiring new fans and players. A family? No, there is a harder edge than familial unconditional love.

Pragmatic swansongs

Occasionally, a current selector (a relatively unflashy role in the grand scheme) has to take a position about a truly world-class career – one of the city state's great heroes.

During the 2018 summer, former captain and record run scorer Alastair Cook decided he would retire from Test cricket at the end of the series against India. Though I'd long sensed what Cook was planning, he only formally told the team and management that he wouldn't play beyond the India series after the victory in the 4th Test at the Ageas Bowl.

I have huge respect for Cook. But I thought two things needed rational consideration before announcing the squad for the 5th and final Test. What was his state of mind about playing in the finishing match of the summer? And second, did he still command a place in the team on merit? Put differently, I didn't think we should select Cook – however great a player he had been – on the grounds that 'he deserved a swansong', especially if he had, emotionally, already 'moved on' to the next phase of his life and career.

When I was in discussions with coaches about Cook's retirement, I sensed they were a little coy about when they first heard the news, and concerned about what I was thinking and planning. If people thought we were even contemplating being so ruthless as to drop Cook for his 161st and final Test then I was

... well ... delighted. We had no intention of doing so, but I wasn't against the principle of considering it.

As it turned out, all the decision-makers agreed that Cook the player, all things being equal, did warrant a place in the team at the Oval. But there was one more thing I wanted to know: what was Cook's state of mind?

I called him the day before the squad was announced. I'd decided to be as lightly inquisitive as I could, as though the issue was nicely open-ended and far from settled. How did he feel about playing at the Oval? Did he still feel motivated now he was certainly going to retire?

Cook, as tough-minded and principled as ever, instantly understood what I was getting at. He said he had huge pride in his performance and that he wanted to play in the 5th Test. He quickly added that if the selectors felt differently and didn't select him – and looked to the future straight away – he would totally understand. He repeated this several times. If we didn't select him, he would understand. But he was up for the challenge; very much up for the challenge. There was absolutely no sense of entitlement in the way Cook approached the conversation: he wanted to play, but he never even hinted that it was his right.

In fact, I had wanted Cook to feel that I'd initially been open-minded, and then, as he'd been so determined and assertive about pride in his performance, that the whole issue had clarified well for everyone. A seriousness had entered Cook's voice that I hadn't heard for a while. He was really up for it, I intimated at the end of the call; that was all we needed to know.

After the phone call, Cook returned to his round of golf with James Anderson. And he was true to his word about the 5th

Test. Cook made an imperious century and England won the Test. For Cook, the standing ovations kept coming.

Watching Cook's glorious farewell, one of the happiest England Tests, was another reminder that farewells are always better when they suit the whole team, not just the individual. Cook had offered the selectors the option of backing a younger player. We'd trusted him to dig deep one last time. Both perspectives, in different ways, had put England first.

Cautionary Instincts

In the absence of an overarching theoretical 'policy', there are only judgements. So an important habit, after the result has come in, is that of looking at the judgements we made: what could we have done differently and better? That question, of course, quickly yields to a second: what could we have done differently and better *with the information we had at the time*? In other words, which 'mistakes' hold as 'true mistakes', *without relying on the benefit of hindsight*?

Here is one. In late July 2019, England set out on a new sequence of Test matches, including an Ashes campaign, only *10 days* after Jofra Archer's Super Over. This brutally abbreviated turnaround between marquee events was one of the hardest challenges of the whole three years. Players and management who'd been part of the World Cup journey were mentally and physically exhausted. Those who hadn't been part of the World Cup triumph inevitably wondered what it had been like.

One of those entering the arena was James Anderson, England's greatest bowler and now a Test match specialist.

Anderson was returning from injury and had missed the Test match against Ireland immediately before the Ashes series against Australia.

Anderson was medically cleared as fit to play in the 1st Ashes Test at Edgbaston. But after four miserly overs in the 1st innings (3 maidens, 1 run), he limped off injured. He did not return. There is no worse time to lose a player to injury than at the very start of a match. A bowler down, England lost the Test match by 251 runs – the worst possible start to the series. It was a good effort by Joe Root's team to claw back to 2–2 across the five matches.

Here is Mike Atherton's painfully clear analysis from his daily match report in *The Times*:

> The medical staff and selectors will have some tricky questions to answer, too, given that Anderson had no chance to prove his match fitness and his readiness was taken on trust. In this there is an echo of the Pakistan series three years ago, when the selectors were lambasted for taking a more cautious approach, having omitted Anderson for the Lord's Test despite the protestations of the bowler and management. Given yesterday's events, you could see why their caution was justified then.

Atherton is playing the ball here (process), not the man (me). And now, with the benefit of perspective – but not relying on hindsight – I can see how we might have done more to avoid what happened.

Could I have taken precaution to the point of paranoia? Could I, with the rest of England cricket riding a euphoric wave, have made it my personal mission to spend the whole week being the most annoying colleague in the whole organisation by asking question after question, continually checking up on the whole process and protocol around this particular return from injury? Could I have taken personal responsibility for making sure that the most uncomfortable conversations – between player, medics, coaches and selectors – were happening with total rigour?

I could. In retrospect I wish I had.

Anderson is a gritty competitor who has navigated matches through serious pain on countless occasions. But even he couldn't do it this time. Champion players, more often than not, want to play, and will back themselves to get through. But the Test match turned out to be a painful lesson in why you need cautionary instincts and processes, too. We made mistakes that week, and it cost England dearly.

Transparency

Two final and connected points about the difficulty of 'policy'.

I take issue with two clichés. First, that transparency is necessarily a good thing. Second, that 'communication' is an end in itself, to be applauded on principle. Both, in fact, demand balance and proportion.

Do you trust anyone who says, 'I'm going to be completely transparent with you'? Didn't think so. 'Complete transparency' is for complete fools or very good liars. In truth, you need sufficient transparency to let enough light in; and sufficient discretion to allow people to take risks and experiment with half-formed ideas in private. A completely transparent selection system would open up all selection meetings to the public via live-streaming. And what would happen then? We know, because some organisations do something similar. The decision-makers simply retreat to written scripts. There is no debate at all. Nothing gets decided at the meeting; individual positions are pre-crafted and then 'announced'. The decision-makers become totally risk-averse when the cameras are rolling (it is only natural and sensible to be so).

Further, the real meeting – that is, the place where ideas and decisions are debated – simply moves into a different and (private) forum. The more you abolish the back door, Tom Wolfe quipped, the more you create the need to reinvent it.

A second rule of thumb: if someone says their job is 'all about communication' they are bad at decision-making. Interesting jobs are about making better decisions, decisions which then demand effective communication. It should be that way around: the primacy of the decision, leading to effective communication. It's tempting for leaders to communicate far too much externally: they like to be 'in the media' but with no effect beyond devaluing their words.

'Never "do" the media without an announcement to make,' a wise old financier advised me when I started as selector. If you have a real decision to communicate – a team has been picked, for example – you'll obviously be able to explain it. If you don't have anything substantive to say, stay out of view. Less and more disciplined communication is part of a broader philosophy: be long-term. You might even call it a policy.

When the facts change

Despite my reservations about 'policy', I became associated with a very controversial one: 'rotation policy'.

At the end of 2020, the last set of selection decisions I was involved in, this was England's upcoming playing schedule (January 2021 to the end of March 2022) in comparison with our closest rivals (Australia, India and New Zealand):

Match days:
England – 145
India – 84
NZ – 65
Australia – 45

That equates to the following days spent on tour:

England – 374
India – 207
NZ – 154
Australia – 128

Over the 453-day period (January 2021–March 2022), England's schedule meant they were 'on tour' 83 per cent of the time.

If Manchester City played three times as much as Liverpool, would Pep Guardiola adopt the same player management strategies as Jürgen Klopp? Of course he wouldn't. Any sensible manager would devise an approach to player management that was suited to the particular circumstances facing his team.

On top of the sheer volume of cricket, Covid added further complications. First, recurrent quarantine periods had both mental and physical repercussions. Second, being almost permanently on tour while having to remain inside a Covid 'bubble' (hotel room ... cricket dressing room ... hotel room ... repeat, indefinitely ...) created compound risks, even for the most psychologically resilient players.

At the start of 2021 – a year that began with the team spending three unbroken months inside totally sealed-off Covid 'bubbles' in Sri Lanka and India – we decided to manage these unique circumstances proactively. The selectors pledged that each of the multi-format players (Ben Stokes, Jofra Archer, Jos Buttler, Jonny Bairstow, Moeen Ali, Mark Wood and Sam Curran) would be given a block of rest outside the bio-secure environment of the tour – time to recharge at home in the UK, in the more normal living conditions of the civilian world.

As a result of that policy, it was unavoidable that some players would leave the squad, and others would join, in the middle of a series. That is imperfect – highly imperfect. But we felt the alternative – the same players remaining inside Covid 'bubbles' throughout the schedule – brought greater risks, for the team as well as for individual players.

We honoured our word that no player would be expected to stay inside a bio-secure bubble for three months straight. Results started well. Powered by record-breaking performances by Joe Root, England won both Tests in Sri Lanka. The team continued the winning streak in the 1st Test against India at Chennai. But the rest of the Test tour, played on pitches that spun markedly, proved exceptionally difficult and India ran away with the last three Tests, completing a 3–1 series win.

Losing 3–1, while making so many selection changes, was interpreted in many quarters as a refutation of rotating the squad. Everyone could see that the strains and complications of Covid had created a puzzle that was hard to resolve. But when you lose, strategy is perceived to have failed; it can feel futile to argue against the wind. The 'rest and rotation' policy became a lightning rod for disappointments about the tour.

But was 'rotation' the central factor in defeat by India? On the previous tour to India – no Covid, no rotation – England had lost 4–0, not 3–1. The final three defeats also clouded the Test team's relative success in overseas conditions across three consecutive winters – posting Test results of four wins and two defeats in 2018–19, three wins and two defeats in 2019–20, and now three wins and three defeats in 2020–21.

We didn't get everything right during those difficult Covid cricket tours. But as I write, leading players in rival teams – such as Virat Kohli for India and David Warner for Australia – are not playing for their respective national team. They are being rested. Aaron Finch, Australia's white-ball captain, pointed to England's approach as an example that other countries would have to follow if Covid restrictions continued.

Perhaps we could have done better at explaining the challenges – the compound effect of the schedule and Covid restrictions – to the wider public. I tried to do this in every selection press conference. But clearly not well enough.

The landscape had changed. Covid was part of this, but there were also underlying shifts. The old problem (England's top talent playing too much for their counties) had been largely resolved by the introduction of England central contracts from 1999 onwards.* A newer problem, with the expansion in the number of formats and the sheer quantity of cricket, was that England's multi-format players might now end up playing too much for England. We needed a wider pool of players to cope, not a smaller one.

The facts had changed, and decisions had to serve new realities. The solutions for 1999 didn't fit for 2021. It wasn't possible to imprison 11 players in a Covid bubble indefinitely and play them into the ground – and out of their minds.

Some critics argued that the rotation policy unfairly favoured the T20 and ODI teams above the Test team. In fact, during the Covid pandemic – and throughout the whole three years – we tried to deploy players so that England succeeded in all three formats simultaneously.

The win–loss ratio for Eoin Morgan's and Joe Root's teams from spring 2018 to spring 2021 were very similar:

The Test team won 21 and lost 12.
The ODI side won 30 and lost 14.
The T20 team won 20 and lost 10.

Whatever the format, England's chances of winning the match stayed fairly consistent (roughly seven wins out of 10) – the only period in the history of England cricket when all three formats have been successful simultaneously. England also enjoyed a

* Central contracts – which contracted leading players directly to the ECB rather than their county teams – gave England's management more control over England players.

winning record against every other team they played during that three-year period. In every rivalry (England vs India, England vs Australia, England vs New Zealand ...) England led overall.

Some of this deeper success got lost amid the unique challenges of trying to keep players sane and performing well in a relentless schedule further complicated by the strain of Covid.

England adopted a progressive approach, and results were broadly successful. But the facts were sometimes drowned out by the noise. With decision-making, that can go with the territory.

9
Process/ Anti-Process

'I've always felt committee meetings tend to last as long as the person who wants them to last the longest wants them to last,' the investor Howard Marks noted. 'Since that's never me, they make me impatient (unless they're doing really interesting stuff).' Me too. Which is why people who like meetings shouldn't be allowed to call them. And why as soon as the meeting stops being important or useful, it has to be stopped.

Impatience is usually framed as a criticism. But I don't know a single person of ability who isn't impatient – impatient to get past the waffle and into the content. Impatience is a precious resource.

So the art of effective meetings, and effective process more generally, is to nudge people and systems towards an enhanced time-to-content ratio: more insight and collaboration per minute. If you want to run a successful team, it helps to treat everyone with respect – beginning with respect for their time. Wasting a colleague's time is the surest way to make them less effective and co-operative.

We wanted our meetings about selection to be thorough and open-minded, but also plain-spoken and decisive. The goal was directness, clarity and unfussy debate about the most important issues. Towards that end, 'a good process' can be helpful. But process should never provide a convenient refuge for people who want to hide from clear debate and sound judgement. The goal is improving judgement, not creating tiers upon tiers of process. Process is the facilitator, not the master.

Above all, as the second half of this chapter explores, meetings and process must be stopped from eating into the infinitely harder (and rarer) activity of thinking and looking at things with fresh eyes.

In other words, for every good process you also need a good *anti-process*. If you are going to follow a series of steps, you need to make sure you're not only following a series of steps. That paradox is central to good decision-making.

'Many eyes, many times'

A good decision-making system rests on two distinct components: better information and superior interpretation of that information.

In pursuit of the first, we wanted potential England players to be judged and assessed by 'many eyes, many times'. *Expert eyes.* A network of scouts across the country focused intensely on watching, assessing and reporting on the next-in-line England players. The Talent ID department then aggregated these *subjective but expert judgements.* (Remember: non-scientific judgements are not necessarily 'punts'.) That was one category of information that fed into me and the other selectors.

The creation of this scouting network took years of hard work. In 2011, Mo Bobat, a former teacher in his mid-twenties with a sharp interest in coaching and skill acquisition, was recruited into the ECB by Simon Timpson (now Performance Director at Manchester City).

From the beginning of his time at the ECB, as Mo studied coaching sessions and devised training programmes across England cricket, he couldn't banish a heretical set of questions from his mind: were cricket coaches actually effective at identifying which players would go on and 'make it'?

Nearly all cricket's resources were focused on coaches and coaching, with little funding or attention given to expertise in recruitment and identification of talent (Talent ID). Across the whole game, status, money and decision-making authority was mainly or wholly in the hands of coaches. There were two assumptions within this imbalance: first, that coaching had a bigger impact on performance than effective selection and Talent ID (big question mark there); second, that the best coaches were the best identifiers of talent anyway (even bigger question mark).

Further, might the two skills – coaching and selection – even be partly conflicted? After all, coaches naturally find that some players respond to them better than others. And it's incredibly hard to be indifferent to these personal biases in making selection decisions. In asking coaches to do all selection, cricket was asking teachers to also be examiners. Who could blame coaches if they tilted towards those who cared more and tried harder? (Not to mention those players who flattered and charmed them.) But that's not the job of an examiner. 'How deserving is he?' shouldn't undermine 'How good is he?' After all, a sports scoreboard, like an academic exam, captures performance – not effort.

Could independent eyes – freed from the distraction of wondering how decisions would impact their daily life at the chalk-face of cricket practice – discover different players, who were currently being undervalued by coaches? Clearly, coaching was very important in its own terms – Mo had once wanted to be one himself – but what if a cricket team could be transformed by different levers: the people who assessed talent, before deciding on apportioning opportunity? In other words: scouting and selection.

Combining insights from behavioural science with models adapted from football and American sport, Mo designed a network of independent and expert scouts across England. He began his experiment at a level down from elite cricket – across the Under-19s age group. Mo was now capturing scouting assessments of every promising player across the country in a centralised database for the whole of England cricket.

Just as analyst Nathan Leamon didn't think data was the silver bullet that fixed everything, Mo didn't believe that scouting information was the only relevant or decisive form of information. Scouting reports needed to be carefully weighed and balanced alongside coaching insights and performance data in developing a complete picture for every player – information that could inform better selection.

Mo persuaded the England MD Andrew Strauss of this point: Talent ID needed to be embedded not only at the level of the U-19 England team, but at the very top of the game. Having created the Talent ID department inside England cricket, Mo now set about merging his new scouting systems with one of the oldest offices inside English cricket: selection.

Effectively, two departments came together – the traditional selection department, and the new Talent ID department – with one person at the sharp end required to filter, weigh, make and communicate decisions (for the role they ended up recruiting me to do, working in tandem with James Taylor).

The new independent selection system, launched in spring 2018, was therefore simultaneously a restoration and a revolution. It was a restoration of cricket's oldest traditions, in which the selectors (independent and outside the dressing room) aimed to choose players wisely for the on-field boss, the captain. But the new system was also revolutionary in terms of advancing how to capture, evaluate and draw on scouting information and data insights. (Several Premier League teams asked Mo and me to present to them about the systems we used.)

This was a paradox of the 2018–21 period. It was easy to present the very role of selector at this time as an anachronism – a throwback to the pre-coaching days when selectors in blazers strolled around the corridors of power. Easy but misleading. England's new investment in recruitment brought it in line with the most progressive sports organisations in football and American sports, where the back office (general managers, chief scouts, analysts) were holding ever greater influence over strategy and decision-making. And winning more games as a result. The new system, in other words, was both intrinsic to cricket and also in line with how sport in general was moving forward.

Above all, the new system's independence (independent from counties, independent from coaching, independent from conflicts of interest) was bound up with its authority. It sounds pretentious, but it was a little like the independence achieved by the Bank of England in 1997: an established institutional tradition was awarded fresh authority by being able to define its own terms.

The new system, as always, relied on personal collaboration as well as definable processes. Mo and I formed a natural partnership: Mo was a brilliant organiser who had created much of the infrastructure; I had always enjoyed making decisions and thinking independently. But there was overlap as well as differing expertise. While running the machine smoothly, Mo was also a strategic thinker; I was a decision-maker, but also interested in organisational efficiency. In tandem, we covered a decent amount of ground.

There is a final point about scouting within the selection process. The selectors never hid behind 'what the scouts said' any more than we hid behind 'what the data said'. Instead, we consulted different categories of evidence – performance data, coaching insights, the expert testimony of scouts – and then drew our own conclusions.

The process

There were several stages in the scouting process.

First, we asked each of the 18 counties to nominate players who they believed warranted England consideration (around 100 'long-listed' players who we would filter down to about 70), providing a broad map of perceived talent and potential. At the first scouting meeting of the year, this long list was whittled down to players of close interest (around 50) who were assessed according to pre-identified characteristics and skills (in line with England's needs). The scouts' findings and assessments (plus video footage and key performance data) were aggregated and curated on an App available to all England's coaches and selectors.

Alongside informal debate across the season, twice a year we held scouting meetings at England's Performance Centre in Loughborough, where the selectors and scouts debated the assessment and rankings of players. The second of these meetings, in late August or early September, was scheduled just before the final meeting of the year: the selection of the winter touring squads

England's scouts were highly diverse. At one end of the spectrum were some of the 'wise old men' of English cricket, who had played as far back as the 1950s and 1960s. At the other end, we drew on the insights of Ajmal Shahzad (retired 2017), as well as James Foster and Jonathan Trott, who were both still active county players in 2018 (before moving into coaching roles). Having modern players acting as scouts – combined with the wider perspective of wise owls who'd seen it all – gave scouting meetings breadth and texture. During my years as selector, we continued to add expertise into the scouting network – including Alec Stewart, 133 Tests for England, and Sir Alastair Cook, 161 Tests for England (and still turning out for Essex).

James Taylor, appointed as the second independent selector in July 2018, was also a central part of scouting debate as well as the final selection decision. James was totally connected to the current generation of players, and understood the incentives and dilemmas that face modern cricketers. James's playing experiences also gave him distinct perspective. For many people in decision-making roles, 'biases' are abstract concepts found in behavioural economics. When James was a player, 'bias' was a daily experience – and not in a good way. 5ft 6 tall (in thick socks), James was the shortest England player of his generation. As a batter, plenty of pundits discounted him as a prospect even before they'd seen him play. As a selector, James wasn't likely to be misled by what players looked like or whom they resembled (what the psychologists Daniel Kahneman and Amos Tversky called the 'representativeness bias'). He was interested in substance.

Selection meetings

At some meetings, we were at the beginning of a new cycle and needed to argue from first principles. On other occasions, for example in the middle of a series with the parameters already set, we were looking at a narrower question – a tactical switch, or replacing one player with another on a like-for-like basis. For that reason, one of the most important decisions in any meeting is deciding what kind of meeting it is.

But while each meeting always had its own context, there were consistent frameworks and inputs that fed into every selection process.

Deciding on priorities. There were phases when England had to select entirely separate squads for different formats simultaneously – which obviously demanded making choices about priorities, especially where to deploy multi-format players. During the 'Covid' summer of 2020, for example, the Test 'bubble' formed first, and took priority over the ODI and T20 squads that assembled later in the season.

Physical and psychological assessments. The Science and Medicine Department provided assessments of all players under discussion, both in terms of injury and also mental health/well-being (especially important when players faced months inside bio-secure Covid bubbles, cut off from the outside world).

Performance data. Analysis included player head-to-heads in particular positions under discussion, weighted averages for next-in-line players, and also insights about upcoming opponents and venues and how that might influence our team formation.

Scouting. The head of Talent ID (first Mo Bobat, then David Court when he joined the ECB from the Football Association in 2020) provided aggregated scouting insights for all players under review. One example of a clear 'winner' from scouting was Ollie Robinson, who routinely ranked highly among the experts who watched him closely, long before Robinson came into mainstream debate. Robinson's early success for England in Test cricket, which was in line with the scouting judgements, was a testament to the Talent ID system (the information providers) more than the selectors (the decision-makers). If I was being self-critical, Robinson could have been selected earlier than his first inclusion in an England Test squad, which came during the West Indies series in 2020. (Even then, he had to wait a bit longer before making it into a final XI.)

The next point can't be stressed enough: these early stages of the meeting were designed to make sure the selectors weren't missing anything. But having good information doesn't (and never will) guarantee making good decisions. Superior information can help, but it can't decide.

Our medics, psychologists and analysts would work right up to the hour of the meeting to give us the best and most up-to-date information. I trusted the information, and I think selection as a whole benefited from the process. But even writing down the various stages of the meeting, as I have here, shouldn't create a false equivalence. Because the last part was the critical dimension: **debate and final decision**.

In my time, there were three 'voting' selectors: two independent selectors (James and me), plus the head coach (initially Trevor Bayliss, then Chris Silverwood). In truth, there wasn't an occasion when an actual vote was required between the three selectors. By the end of the conversation, it was clear where consensus lay.

We also invited the team captain – Joe Root for Test selection and Eoin Morgan for ODI and T20 selections – to every selection meeting. Though he wasn't technically a voting selector, we all felt that the captain should be present as he is a central figure in every aspect of team strategy. That blend – the captain always there and often influential, but not strictly accountable for squad selections – seemed a good balance, given that the captain is also a teammate and peer of the players under discussion. As I learnt in my own captaincy days, sometimes you can have too much direct accountability for every decision.

Meetings come alive when different kinds of insights are brought to the table, not just differing opinions. The best meetings combined both the inside view – which the coach and captain could bring from their immersive observation of players in the dressing room – and also the 'outside' perspective that comes from being one step removed from the sweat and tears of day-to-day team life, a potential advantage for independent selectors, who watch with some emotional distance (albeit deep investment).

After the squad had been selected, there was one more important task: deciding on internal communication for selected and deselected players, and also finalising our external messaging, which I would usually present to the media at a press conference the following day.

Our rule was that the player should be the first to find out about any 'change in status' (whether 'in' or 'out' of the Test, ODI or T20 squad). This policy meant that many selection meetings ended in a large number of confidential and urgent phone calls. To minimise leaks, you had to move fast.

Anti-process

Every decision-making process is by definition institutional: it takes place within an organisation, with inputs from many sources of information across several departments, feeding into several decision-makers. And yet the process, if it's going to work well, relies on those decision-makers retaining fierce individuality, even when they are playing as part of a team.

This echoes the concept of 'uninstitutional behaviour' in Chapter 2. A central leadership challenge is nudging colleagues and fellow decision-makers to strive for original insights, rather than safely herding them along the train-tracks of compliance and conformity. A process, in other words, is only as good as the anti-process alongside it.

First, you can be too prepared for a meeting as well as too under-prepared. Eliminating spontaneity from a process usually derives from a lack of intellectual self-confidence. In contrast, a confident chair will always back themselves to get the meeting back on track after an interesting digression or tangent.

An effective meeting teases out live thoughts, not stillborn pronouncements. If you tie it all up too much in advance, there's no scope for new insights. 'No surprise in the writer,' reflected the poet Robert Frost, 'no surprise in the reader.'

A related fallacy is that a good decision-maker always knows exactly how the decision-making process is going to end up (in this analysis, the central figure simply 'manages' everyone else in the meeting or committee towards his predetermined destination). Much better – while retaining a loose sense of which outcomes are attractive – to retain room for openness and discovery, which in turn rest on scepticism and genuine debate. 'Thinking is nothing but talking to yourself inside,' argued Richard Feynman. A good decision-making process encourages the protagonists to speak without editing out all the risky bits.

I worked with two renowned newspaper editors. One tended to call formal meetings at which people straightened their backs and sounded impressive. The other editor just popped up at surprising moments and asked disarming questions – so you ended up saying what you thought before you'd had a chance to make it all sound grander and more reasoned than it was. He mastered the art of benevolent ambush, and it allowed him to find out what people – of all ranks in the newspaper – really believed. Central to this gift was eliminating the fear of being 'caught out': no spontaneous or truthful opinion was ever 'held against you'. It is a huge gift to bring this mood of incautious honesty and discovery into formal meetings, too: retaining, in other words, the spirit of a conversation rather than a courtroom.

And a good conversation about an important topic brings the probability of tension. Though our selection meetings were courteous, I agree with the investor Barton Biggs that 'harmonious, happy meetings may be a warning of groupthink and complacency, whereas agitation, passionate arguments and some stress are good signs'.

In a good meeting, even though there is an ultimate authority who accepts responsibility, ideas and arguments should stand or fall on their own merit. 'What decision would you make *if you were the only decision-maker*?' That was a phrase I used to prompt colleagues to tease out what they really thought. Your job, if you are running the meeting, is to get to the points of difference, and then resolve them to a satisfactory degree. You have to find the discord in order to reconcile it. If you don't find it (assuming it exists), then you've just kicked the can down the road. Cosiness kills effective decision-making. Irving Janis, who coined the term 'group think', advocated an atmosphere of 'intellectual suspicion amid personal trust'. Thought patterns which begin, 'Well, obviously we aren't going to …' are starting in the wrong place.

Which is why you shouldn't set out to compromise, but instead to seek solutions – because there might be a new and clear solution which doesn't demand a compromise. Compromise – or proportion – might (or might not) be the consequence, but it shouldn't be the founding ambition.*

Just as important as getting to other people's beliefs is the ability to ambush *yourself*: can you find techniques to refresh your own opinions as well? This gets harder as people get more senior and busier. And it's a major problem. The tendency is to become rehearsed and entrenched, rather than curious and open.

* 'No, truth, being alive, was not half-way between anything … It was only to be found by continuous excursions into either realm, and though proportion is the final secret, to espouse it at the outset is to ensure sterility' – E. M. Forster, *Howard's End* (1910).

Can you put yourself in the way of surprise? We go to bookshops partly to benefit from happy chance finds: in looking for the book we think we want, we find the book we didn't know we wanted. The near-miss is actually the bullseye. It's the same with newspapers. A great editor can do something Google cannot. He or she puts the story you didn't know you wanted to read – the story your tastes and preferences do not predict – next to the one you thought you wanted to read. A newspaper is the carefully curated art of serendipity. Like a thoughtful host at a party, an editor expands our lives by creating surprise.

The skilful bookshop owner and the gifted editor have lessons for our professional lives as well as our pleasures. Can you make connections other people cannot? Can you identify a helpful analogy? Will you bring an outsider's perspective? Can you reconfigure existing information in a new and original way? Can you take one position while still inhabiting the counterfactual worlds of positions not taken? Can you play with a problem as well as persist with it? Put simply, can you avoid being drowned by the bureaucratic swamp? The answers to those questions will be bound up with the quality of your decisions.

I certainly didn't always succeed. While I was researching this book, I reread three years' of my England notebooks from 2018 to 2021. If there was an overall trajectory, I found they got more bogged down with irrelevant subjects ('the system'), and slightly less focused on solutions. You have to stay close to the vision of that outsider who initially sees things clearly, with no loyalties or attachments.

In previous books, I've touched on the downsides of ultra-professionalism when it is badly interpreted (fearfulness, presenteeism, hoop-jumping, form-filling, cliché, process-obsessiveness, management waffle). In the two decades since first framing the argument, those trends have got even worse, contributing to decision-making processes becoming unwieldy and interminable.

Drawing on your personal observations of the working world, ask yourself this question. What proportion of your company/organisation's time is wasted on a version of the following tendency: 'If, one day, we need to *make it look like* we'd done this task thoroughly and "professionally", how would we dress up the process to make it look really serious?'

Making it look good in case it all goes wrong – in slang, 'arse-covering' – has been on the march. When the term 'process' is used in this context, the concept has nothing to do with making better decisions. Process, in effect, is being positioned so it can be put in a drawer and wheeled out retrospectively, if required. Process becomes a kind of insurance policy against future scrutiny: an expensive and wasteful insurance policy.

Time for the fight-back. If you want to improve actual performance rather than just fill up time, you'll need to help decision-makers to avoid 'going under' to 'process', and instead devote their energy on thinking hard and seeking good ideas.

This challenge got even harder with Covid, as video-conferencing became more frictionless, and the temptation to call irrelevant and unproductive meetings became irresistible. People who found that having time on their hands led to feelings of insecurity and doubt had a ready solution: call a meeting!

The definitive dimension of a process is the energy, care, liveliness, disinterestedness, openness, freshness and mischief – the *life* – of the people who inform and direct it. In taking a penalty, deciding where you're aiming is only part of the story; then you've got to kick.

I wanted our selection process to be so rigorous that we never had to waste any energy on trying to look rigorous. And that rested on keeping the spirit of anti-process central to the process – just as the best professionals retain a splash of the amateur's detachment, however high the stakes become.

10
X-Ray Cricket

In the autumn of 2003, on a freezing evening in Cambridge, Massachusetts, I paused outside the window of the Harvard bookstore, stopped in my tracks by a book advert: 'How the scientific method revolutionized professional baseball.' I bought a copy and wrote the first review of the book in England. It was *Moneyball*, Michael Lewis's exploration of how the Oakland As, powered by smart data, punched far above their wealth and status. A financially poor team had thought its way (rather than bought its way) to baseball's top table.

As well as being a book and film, over the last 20 years 'Moneyball' has also become a kind of slogan for data-informed strategy across all sports, sometimes pejorative, sometimes admiring. Managers and strategists who 'believe in data' have searched for new areas of sport that could be 'Moneyballed', shorthand for 'progressive' and 'evidence-based'. And critics, who dislike the idea of data as a dominant factor in sport, have enjoyed looking out for data-led strategies or tactics which went wrong. These are then ridiculed as 'over-engineered' or lacking in 'good old common sense'.*

A constituency in modern sport likes the idea that data holds the answers. And there is a different constituency (larger, it must be said) which thinks that innovative thinkers (especially data-informed ones) are more often the problem than the solution. So Moneyball became a conceptual football kicked about between adversaries inside sport's culture wars. 'Data/Moneyball – what a load of rubbish!' 'Data/Moneyball – always the way forward!' As always with culture wars, first take an aggressive position, then find out what we are talking about.

But there was a central misconception about the applicability of Moneyball to the selection of England teams. Moneyball was only partly about data, much more about price. The Oakland As exploited the fact that rival teams were misunderstanding true value in terms of on-field contribution, inevitably leading them to make mistakes about the pricing of players. If you measure the wrong things, then you misjudge players' true contribution and hence misprice them. Conversely, if you are able to see through the wrapper of inflated reputation and get past the false advertising, you're going to buy products at more efficient prices. The Oakland As capitalised on these inefficiencies and sold players who were overpriced and bought players who were underpriced. That's why the Oakland As, financially poor by baseball standards, outperformed much wealthier rivals.

---

* Basketball legend Charles Barkley put it like this: 'These guys who talk about analytics, they're a bunch of guys who ain't never played the game, and they never got the girls in high school and they just want to get in the game.'

But whereas teams like the Oakland As are constantly engaged in trading players with rival teams, England cricket, of course, is a national sports team which *cannot* buy and sell players. England couldn't sell Ben Stokes (not that anyone would want to) to Australia any more than we could buy Virat Kohli from India. In international cricket selection, there is no transfer market.

In other words, and this is a central point, in international cricket there is no fluidity of talent *between* teams, only *within* teams. It doesn't ultimately matter, from a strategic or decision-making point of view, how you rate your own talent against that of the opposition. They have theirs, and you have yours, and there is no room for negotiation or exchange. Simply, there is no market.

In the absence of a transfer market, your scope in cricket is very different. You can rank your own players in ways that differ from conventional wisdom. And you can assemble the pieces into a differently configured whole that fits the current context. Both challenges are fascinating and difficult, but they are the central levers of influence. Put simply, data is most useful for an England selector when it leads you to re-evaluate the reputation of existing talent, or when it helps you to understand the team's needs more fully and efficiently. That's very different from a trading strategy based on a contrarian view about price.

What's 'good'?

'He/she is superb/awful/underrated/pathetic.' To which the only answer is: superb/awful/underrated/pathetic *relative to whom*? Yet this essential clause, which warrants a place in every debate about any player (or employee), is usually notable by its absence.

Amid the opinions, you also need some cool, dispassionate context. And it's here that data can definitely help. What's normal? What's in line with reasonable performance? What is the baseline trend? And if circumstances are distorting rational expectations, how can you use data to bring language – and decision-making – back into line with reality?

During my first couple of years as a selector, all Test sides found batting in English conditions extremely difficult. So it was easy to misinterpret what 'normal' really looked like. Another brilliant bowling display by England/the opposition … and another awful batting performance by England/the opposition. But if all batting teams are routinely described as 'useless' and all bowling sides are called 'brilliant', shouldn't terms like 'useless' and 'brilliant' be reassessed? I thought so.

At the end of summer of 2019, I aggregated the bowling averages of all the different teams who'd played Tests in England into one table, to provide some context for discussions we were having about the relative performance of batters and bowlers in English conditions.

Across the two years I'd been selector (2018 and 2019), seam bowlers from all countries who'd played Tests in England had these bowling averages:

9.66
10.83
12.28
14.20
16.33
18.42
19.62
20.27
20.94
21.28
21.85
22.21
22.75
24.27
24.66
24.66
24.70
25.33
25.92
29.75
31.50
31.83
33.40
33.72
38.87
40.5
42.14
53.5

For me, as an ex-batter, the central point couldn't be more obvious: that is a *scary* set of bowling averages. With so many bowlers averaging in the 20s or lower, the ball, very clearly, is dominating the bat. In this context, a bowling average in the low 20s was actually pretty standard.*

Now let's take these simple and publicly available numbers and see how they are relevant to a hypothetical discussion about selection in the real world of people and emotions.

Suppose a bowler was dropped from the team despite having a bowling average in recent matches of, say, 26. (Sorry to disappoint, but hypothetical here really is hypothetical.) 'You can't possibly drop me,' he could argue, 'I'm taking my

---

* Far from sophisticated data analytics – the sample size varies significantly across the different teams and is sometimes very small – the list is purely illustrative.

wickets at 26! This is outrageous – 26 is a world-class bowling average!'

And, of course, taken over a whole career and in all conditions around the world, 26 is indeed a world-class bowling average. But for matches played in England during the period under review, 26 is actually well *below* the median performance for specialist seam bowlers. As a benchmark, therefore, a bowling average of 26 is both excellent and relatively moderate at the same time ... *depending entirely on context* – the context of the pitch, the conditions, and the difficulty of scoring runs.

Just as we did for bowlers in the previous section, let's now approach Test match batting performances: what had been 'normal' for Test batters, from all countries, in English conditions?

Further context: during this period, it had become commonplace to single out English batters, especially opening batters, for harsh criticism. Former England captain and pundit Nasser Hussain, when asked whom he would select to play against Australia in 2019, wrote up his team as: 'Opener A, Opener B, Joe Root [rest of the team ...].' He couldn't endorse one opener, let alone two. As the series progressed – including England being bowled out for 67 at Headingley – the question of performance among England's batters dominated cricket debate.

Again, what follows is not intended as high-level 'data analysis'; it is presented just to offer useful context about reasonable expectations.

Here are all the opening batters, ranked by conventional average, who played in the major Test series in England across 2018 and 2019 – England vs Pakistan, England vs India and England vs Australia. (The sample does not include the high-scoring 2018 Test match at the Oval, which was unique in this period

– and 'un-English' – in that the ball did not dominate the bat to the same degree.)

Burns – 33.5
Denly – 28.5
Dhawan – 26.33
Cook – 22.6
Jennings – 19.88
Iman-ul-Haq – 18.67
Azhar Ali – 16.75
K. L. Rahul – 16
Harris – 11.5
Bancroft – 11
Warner – 9.88
Roy – 8.86
M. Vijay – 6.5
Stoneman – 6.5

In total, this sample includes 11 Test matches, featuring 44 individual innings by opening batters: 1,424 runs, 78 dismissals, 18.3 average per dismissal.

That is a remarkable dominance of the ball over the bat. There are some very good batters in that list of low averages, including the highest run scorer in England history (Cook), and a decent proportion of players with an impressive overall Test average of over 40 (Dhawan, Cook, Azhar Ali, Warner). And yet it all adds up to 18.3 per wicket.

So again, in this context, the right question is 'What is normal?' Succeeding as an opening batter in Tests in England (in the conventional sense of a high batting average) was proving too difficult even for very good players. Openers were walking out to bat in English Tests, 'failing' and then (in the case of opposition teams especially) getting dropped from the team. Dhawan, Harris, K. L. Rahul, Bancroft and Vijay were all dropped as openers during the series against England.

Here there was a difference of approach between England and other teams. The only English player to suffer from a 'straight swap' selection (old opener dropped, new opener in) during a series in England was Stoneman. At certain times, there were widespread demands for the selectors to make sacrificial offerings. But the question remained, as it always should: did making a change really improve the team? If not, why do it?

I think we benefited from understanding this context in our handling of the careers of Burns, Denly and Jennings, who all had longish runs in the team. Burns – 23 matches without being dropped; Denly – 15 matches in a row; Jennings – 10 matches. As selectors we were prepared to absorb pressure in support of players who we knew were doing a very difficult job.

In short, just as a bowler might rationally be dropped despite an 'excellent' bowling average of 26, so too a batter might be retained despite a superficially disappointing average in the 20s or low 30s. *Up to a point*, of course. And the shrewd reader will already be using the logic presented here against its author. If it's so difficult to open the batting in England (the superb Australian opener averaged only 9 in 2019), why should any batter lose their place in that context? Shouldn't they get a chance to play in more helpful conditions at the end of the series? This subtle criticism is a far harder case to answer than the superficial 'Why don't you sack the lot of them?!'

Take Jason Roy. It's become a commonplace to argue we made a mistake in selecting Jason, but no one (so far as I know) has made the deeper critique: if the inexperienced Roy did comparably with the experienced Warner in England, didn't Roy deserve the chance to have a crack at opportunities in Test matches overseas (where he might have excelled)? While we, as selectors, take responsibility for the fact that Roy did not get those chances, the logic of the question shifts the debate towards a more enlightening discussion about the difficulty of selecting opening batters in England.

This is not making excuses for batters or avoiding tough decisions. It is about capturing reality. Without a reasonable apprehension of normality, decisions are unlikely to be successful.

Runs should be worth 'more' when batting is hard, and worth 'less' when batting is easy. And the converse is true with bowling: wickets are worth more on flat pitches than in bowler-friendly conditions. Measuring performance, in other words, should be *weighted* according to context and usefulness to the team.

Weighted averages

To help with this challenge, the tool England cricket created was called 'weighted averages'. I'll spare you the algorithm, and instead talk in plain English about principles.

Let's return to the match in which I played against Somerset in 2007, when almost every batter got a hundred. The scorecard reads: Middlesex 1st innings 600/4, Somerset 1st innings 850/7, Middlesex 2nd innings 209/2. The average 'price' of a wicket in this match, therefore, was 128 runs. In that context, my 1st innings score, a nice-sounding 68, wasn't worth very much to the team. In fact, 68 was considerably *below* par, especially for a top-order batter who ought to outperform the average value of a wicket. If you were interested in capturing reality, it would be fair, objectively speaking, to recalibrate my 68 (radically downwards).

Conversely, four years earlier, in the form of my life, I made 108 out of 189 against Essex. The real value of that innings was worth 'more' than 108.

Are runs 'at a premium'? Are wickets 'coming cheap'? These are routine questions in every cricket dressing room in the world. Everyone with common sense in the history of cricket has addressed all these questions intuitively.

Instead of intuition, however, at England cricket we also had an algorithm. Various aspects of match data – including the average runs per wicket in that particular match, the track records of opponents, as well as many other measures – go into the algorithm, which takes each player's traditional or headline score from the innings (the one that is printed in the newspaper) and converts it into a *weighted score*. Cumulatively, these batting scores and bowling analyses – exactly as with 'normal' statistics – are captured as a 'weighted average'.

The algorithm's adjustment doesn't mean the weighted average is *perfectly* representative of a player's value. No system is complete or flawless. It just means the likelihood of being misled by atypical context is reduced. But you're never completely safe from being misled, of course. And you always need to use your judgement.

Overall, weighted averages were helpful because they brought statistics closer to the underlying reality of how much players were contributing to team performance.

Now might come the rejoinder, 'Ah, but over the course of a career, circumstances and contexts average out.' No, they don't.

Because most players – whether it's at county or international level – play roughly half their matches at home, and home conditions vary enormously. A batter from a county with a bowler-friendly home pitch deserves more recognition than headline averages suggest. The same point applies at England level, as the two sets of averages earlier in this chapter reveal.

Weighted averages did not dictate England selection, but they were another useful source of information that helped inform selection. An example when I was grateful to have context built into the data came at the end of the summer in 2019. Going into the last match of the season, just after suffering the disappointment of Australia regaining the Ashes, would we make knee-jerk selection changes for the final Test?

We did not. Jason Roy missed the match due to an injury and team balance: Ben Stokes was not fit to bowl, and so Sam Curran was needed as an extra all-rounder. The other batters all stayed the same.

Throughout the series, there had been considerable media pressure on Joe Denly, now opening the batting, who had a Test average of 25 at that point. But Denly's *weighted* career average was 46. Denly was selected for the 5th Test match and top-scored with 94; England won the match and squared the series 2–2.

Jumping up a level

If one dimension of selection is knowing when to hold on to a player, the opposite question is judging who will make the step up from county cricket to England.

This is extremely difficult, as the two forms of the game – county cricket and international cricket – have been drifting apart in recent years. Just how different are they? Here are some telling comparisons:

Percentage of deliveries over 88 mph:
County – 0.7 per cent
Test – 16.7 per cent

Percentage of wickets falling to spin:
County – 15 per cent
Test – 35 per cent

Percentage of deliveries that are bouncers:
County – 4.6 per cent
Test – 11.1 per cent

In summary: in Test cricket there is much more genuinely fast bowling, more balls are aimed at the batter's head, and spin is far more central.

So in thinking about selecting batters for the next level up, you're always weighing classic questions such as how does a particular batter fare against bowling of over 85 mph? How good is he against world-class spin? How well does he play balls around head height?

In assessing whether a county player is well suited to make the jump up to international level, a judgement needs to be made about the player's character (addressed in Chapter 8, 'Policy?') and also the player's capabilities. Simply, what kind of 'game' do they have?

With bowlers, you are also assessing how county bowlers might fare in the different conditions of Test matches: how successful is he on flatter pitches? When there is less swing? Against better batters?

As we saw in Chapter 5, Jofra Archer was an exceptional case because he was already an established superstar in international franchise cricket. We knew details about every ball he'd bowled in every televised T20 league where he'd played.

Much more often, however, new England players are selected straight from county cricket. Sadly, there is very little HawkEye data from four-day county cricket because it is seldom televised. In county cricket, therefore, no one knows for sure *exactly* how fast people bowled on a particular day, or how many revolutions the spinners put on the ball, or the bounce of the ball on that surface. (All forms of data that are available at every fully televised match.) Hence the challenge for selectors is that they are assessing players for the England team *without* having the insights you get from complete HawkEye data. There is observation and discussion, but no X-ray data vision.

How do you judge who is best suited to making the jump up? This challenge can be helped (though not 'solved') by looking at qualities commonly found in international players who have already succeeded – the attributes of Test match *archetypes*.

Let's consider a specific selection 'journey' for a particular England player. In summer 2020, when cricket resumed after the first Covid lockdown, England's Test squad entered a sealed-off 'bio-secure' environment in Southampton. In the absence of any county cricket, the only preparation for the upcoming series versus West Indies was an internal squad match.

One performance in that internal squad match snuck under the radar in terms of publicity but was very strongly noted by insiders: the contribution of Sussex seamer Ollie Robinson. In the 1st innings (which was Robinson's first taste of being involved with the senior England squad) he recorded figures of 9 overs, 4 maidens, 7 runs and 2 wickets. Robinson looked the real deal, on day one.

Not that Robinson's performance was a surprise to those who had been watching him closely. ('That bloke never misses,' one of the elite coaches at the ground said to me about Robinson's relentless accuracy over dinner that evening.) Instead, Robinson's first run-out in an England shirt *confirmed* what the scouts had been seeing for some time: though yet to achieve full elevation to the England team, Robinson was already playing at the level that more than warranted selection. Further, and this is the interesting part, there was strong evidence that Robinson had the attributes of a bowler who would be well suited to Test cricket, not just county cricket.

Put simply, though it was difficult for a new seam bowler to break into the England team (he'd have to get past Anderson, Broad, Woakes, Archer, Wood and Curran), if Robinson could get an opportunity, it was very likely that he would be Test-match-ready straight away.

Why was there such confidence among selectors and scouts about Robinson? On one level, he was just one of a number of seam bowlers producing spectacular form in county cricket. Across the 2018 and 2019 seasons (the most recent available evidence when that internal match at Southampton was selected), Robinson's bowling average of 18 was very similar to those of Durham's Chris Rushworth and Somerset's Lewis Gregory (both taking their wickets at around 19). Several others, including England squad member Jamie Porter and Yorkshire's Ben Coad, were close behind them. There was a cluster of outstanding wicket-takers.

So why did Robinson stand out as a Test candidate? It wasn't because of pace (Robinson's stock ball is around 80 mph, in line with many bowlers at the top of county cricket). But while speed is one attribute that can help at Test level, it isn't the only attribute. There are three others – **movement**, **accuracy** and (often neglected and forgotten) **release point**.

While Robinson's speed didn't mark him out as different from his county peers, the height from which he delivers the ball was a case apart: Robinson lets the ball go from *17 centimetres higher* than rival leading county bowlers.*

High release point brings innate advantages. Release point equals bounce, and with greater bounce a bowler benefits from a bigger margin of error. Without extra bounce, bowlers find it harder to stop batters attacking their good balls; so pressure grows to bowl the almost perfect ball every time. Second, high release point brings particular advantages in overseas conditions, especially the hard pitches in Australia. There is a reason why the great Australian Glenn McGrath was able to bowl with an old ball in relatively unhelpful conditions: his exceptional release point and laser accuracy starved batters of scoring opportunities and, eventually, batters usually lost the battle of patience and willpower.

Basketball has (too slowly) learnt that while height is obviously an advantage, the greater advantage is *reach*. A player's reach (toes to fingertips) more accurately predicts whether a player will make it to the NBA than just his standing height.

A similar point applies to cricket. *Release point is not the same thing as standing height*. Release point is achieved by the combi-

* Robinson 2.20 metres; Coad 2.03 metres; Gregory 2.0 metres.

nation of height plus bowling action. Some tall bowlers do not have a high bowling action, effectively giving up their physical advantages. But Robinson benefits from both standing height *and* an upright bowling action, creating a compound benefit.

There are two distinct points here. First, though it's not the only path to success, a high release point does make it more likely that a bowler without extreme pace will successfully make the jump up to Test level. High release point is an attacking weapon (creating edges to the slips) as well as a defensive asset (making it harder for batters to score).

Second, in constructing a varied collective bowling attack that can take wickets in all conditions, release point is an underestimated dimension of variety. Left-handedness brings new angle; extreme pace brings physical threat; spin brings guile; and a spread of different release points brings varying types of trajectory and hence bounce. (Mark Wood, who has enjoyed superb days as an England fast bowler, is slight and pacy, with a release point of just 1.85 metres – especially useful when it's mixed in with higher release points.)

Robinson's county performances justified his England selection – but others who *weren't* selected for England also had strong wicket-taking credentials. The decision-makers had so much confidence in Robinson's suitability for Test cricket because his profile fitted a Test match archetype – with his accuracy and high release point suggesting he would bring his prolific Sussex form with him when wearing an England shirt.

As I write this, Robinson has taken 39 Test wickets at an average of 21. That is better than any other current England player. And exactly the same as his county bowling average.

11
Play On

In December 2017, I looked across the outfield at the WACA cricket ground in Perth, watching the Australian captain Steven Smith receive the plaudits for a triumphant win. The series had been wrapped up 3–0, the Ashes had been regained, and Smith, as captain, had been the central protagonist, making scores of 141, 40, 6 and, here in Perth, 239. Smith was 28 years old, the best batter in the world, and had just completed a career-defining success as player and leader. What could be better than this, his finest hour?

Yet the picture in front of us was very different. Smith was giving media interviews – player of the match, victorious captain, Ashes winner … the whole shebang. But he looked anything but happy. His voice was expressionless, as though he was delivering pre-assembled phrases that held no meaning for him. Nor did he look exhausted in a replete way, as top batters sometimes appear after an epic innings. There was something more troubling about Smith's distracted air, absent more than he was present. On the journey from prodigy to champion, had Smith imagined that 'success' would feel like this? Is exhausted numbness the destination where playing cricket, and playing it better than anyone else in the world, should lead?

'Mate, I'm gone'

A few minutes later, away from the cameras, Australia's then chief selector, Greg Chappell, one of the most resilient players of the 1970s and 1980s, bumped into his captain inside the private sanctuary of the dressing room. Chappell reflected on what he saw:

> Steve was sitting on one of the physios' benches staring into space; I walked into the room behind him and he didn't register that anyone was there. I said, 'How are you going?' and he blinked and said, 'Oh mate, I'm gone. I can't sleep, I'm not eating. During a Test I can't do anything. All I can do is play cricket and stagger back to my room.' He was a shell of a man by mid-December and that was a contributing factor to what we saw in South Africa a few months later.

By 'what we saw in South Africa', Chappell is referring to the ball-tampering saga, or 'Sandpaper-gate' – which ended in Australian cricket suffering a crisis that engulfed its central players and leaders.

But there was a lag before the crisis. Immediately after that revealing chat in Perth, Smith continued on, unstoppable. After Chappell had observed a curiously diminished man, Smith carried on where he'd left off – relentlessly blunting England's bowlers with epic stays at the crease. In the 4th Test at Melbourne, Smith made 76 and 102 not out, batting for 11 hours in total. In the 5th and final Test at Sydney, Smith spent another four and a half hours compiling 83. As a sequence of scores, this was superman territory. With the series already won, Smith was still battering the opposition, and rising through the record books at incredible speed. Next ball, next hour, next game, next hundred. It was everything Smith had trained for, and, like a dangerously well-drilled young officer in a war situation, he could only march in one direction.

But Smith was also, it was soon discovered, battering himself. Long running on empty, he was now depleting his reserve tank of emotional fuel to low levels of perspective and, above all, fun.

That was the Smith paradox in 2017–18. Slayer of England … breaker of records … a machine for winning … and yet also an exhausted and increasingly vulnerable human being – a vulnerability that fatefully caught up with him within a few weeks of his 'greatest hour'.

In February 2018, while Smith was captaining Australia against South Africa, the series immediately after he'd triumphed against England, the Australian team used sandpaper to alter the condition of the ball illegally. After a botched denial and then an admission of responsibility, Smith was removed as captain, banned from cricket for 12 months, and precluded from holding any leadership position in Australian cricket for two years. It was a brutal experience for Smith, and whatever the collective failings that went into the initial mistake, it was impossible not to feel deep sympathy for a great sportsman being hounded through an airport, following condemnation from his own prime minister, before breaking down as he apologised in front of the television cameras, standing next to his father. 'I'll regret this for the rest of my life,' Smith said.

I have no wish to add any criticisms at all here – there has been more than enough opprobrium expended already. No, what's interesting is Chappell's analysis, which draws a straight line from Smith's exhaustion and emptiness during the Ashes triumphs ('his mental and physical reserves drained away at a rate of knots', in Chappell's phrase) to the subsequent crisis of Sandpaper-gate ('the other contributing factor in early 2018, in terms of the team's leadership, was that Steve Smith was a shell of his former self'). The captain of a cricket team makes decisions at every level of team life. If he's 'gone', there are hidden risks for the individual, the team and the whole organisation.

Chappell's insights reveal the complex relationship between achievement and long-term sustainability. In this light, some of Smith's pre-South Africa successes are recast as Pyrrhic victories: on one level they were heroic, but it was a heroism that masked various forms of fragility. 'Oh mate, I'm gone' was a warning that went unheeded (as Chappell himself now sees) – understandably, but with consequences.

The machine fallacy

Chad Harbach's novel *The Art of Fielding* (2011), despite its title, gives voice to a widespread and deepening misconception: that sport is best understood as the process of turning vulnerable human beings into cogs in a machine:

> To excel at it [baseball], you had to become a machine ...
> Can you perform on demand, like a car, a furnace, a gun?

It's a trope that runs right through modern sport. 'He's a machine!' has become a term of high approval among fans, coaches and administrators alike.* The metaphor is at best incomplete, and certainly overestimated. And taken to an extreme, it's also dangerous. When people stop thinking they're people, trouble looms.

Even a player's technique is not mechanical. It's an organic process. The surest way for a coach to ruin a player is to 'deconstruct' his game into tiny pieces, pick out one 'cog' that needs improvement, give it a quick bash with the hammer, and then deludedly slot all the pieces back together again. As Manchester City's assistant coach Juanma Lillo quips, 'You can't take an arm off Rafael Nadal and train it separately.'

The machine fallacy is equally flawed at a collective level. Once a team has been misidentified as a machine, all the difficult and important aspects about understanding teams – creativity, play, synergy – can be conveniently ignored. In fact, every successful team relies on the healthy balance of several tensions: between planning and intuition, between structure and freedom, between deliberateness and instinct, between confidence and scepticism, between democracy and command, between discipline and playfulness.

None of those careful balances can be permanently 'fixed', like

---

* That sport corrupts true playfulness has been the suspicion of sport's harshest critics. 'They [sports] ... train men all the more inexorably to serve the machine,' wrote T. W. Adorno in *Dialectic of Enlightenment* (1944), 'hence sports belong to the realm of unfreedom.'

taking a car to the garage. They can only be skilfully maintained. The sign of a healthy team is that while it is always in flux, it never falls too far out of equipoise – always moving, never lurching.

Every context and every team requires a subtly different balance. The best resolution relies in accepting that there can't be a permanent resolution. Mike Brearley tells a story in *The Art of Captaincy* (1985) about a zoo lionkeeper who had a remarkable record in breeding lion cubs, never losing one. Asked for his secret, he replied, 'No two lion cubs are alike.'

Managerialism

Rod Marsh, the iconic 1970s cricketer turned coach and selector, was celebrated among old-school Australian cricket folk for his impatience about the management class's gift for multiplying itself. At one Australian Test trial match, Rod contrasted the sparse backroom staff when he was an aspiring cricketer in the early 1970s (11 players plus a physio, watched and assessed by two selectors), with the relative army of non-playing employees at the same fixture in modern times. One day he counted them all up, before reaching for his phone: 'This is a disgrace! I'm calling Cricket Australia. There are 17 members of management at this game! It's just not fair: they need another manager here to manage them!'

There was a serious point beneath the mischief. Managers tend to appoint more managers so they can manage them, expanding a sense of seniority. In some ways, this trend is like the financialisation of the economy: the financial services sector is now much bigger than the underlying economy. And, again like the financialisation of the economy, each layer of complexity in sport, each new tier of management, brings new risks. 'The system', like any bureaucracy, develops its own needs – and therefore faces problems when those needs are no longer met.

Employees waste their time twice over: first, in trying to demonstrate how they've improved the particular nuts and bolts in their corner of the organisation; second, in attempting to show that if the machine does flop then the fault lies elsewhere on the production line. But what matters, as we've explored earlier, is the way the pieces fit together. In any human business, if 'separate' departments aren't working well co-operatively it's likely to create far bigger problems than if they aren't working well on their own terms.

The machine fallacy finds cover in complexity – sometimes unnecessary complexity. Modern sports organisations, in their pursuit of the next 1 per cent edge, have become more intricate. The support and backroom staff of every top team (across all sports) now significantly outnumber the playing roster. While there have been some real benefits along the way – this book explores how scouting and data analysis can improve teams – there are also profound dangers with the expansion of employees and the diffusion of influence. Paying people to find an edge is rational; paying people to hang around is not.

A complex human system, in the metaphor of the historian Niall Ferguson, starts to resemble a termite hill more than an Egyptian pyramid: 'They operate somewhere between order and disorder ... There comes a moment when complex systems "go critical". A very small trigger can set off a phase transition from a benign equilibrium to a crisis.' This is exactly what happens when sports teams, even formerly great teams, suddenly implode.

Working in elite sport, I've often felt that the team would be more antifragile (and more likely to win) if the management system was simpler, the machine smaller, the language clearer and the atmosphere more playful.

Technique in batting has been well described as 'the best, simplest way'. That holds for organisations, too. Not everything can be simplified. But simplicity should always be the ambition.

Inverse sprezzatura

In 1991, well ahead of his time, the literary critic George Watson called out the underlying problem: the concept of 'work' (not progress, not success, not achievement, just 'work' itself) being recast as a virtue rather than a necessity:

> In earlier ages people overworked, to be sure, but commonly because they were forced by poverty or impelled by a sense of duty. Now work can be a neurotic addiction.

Workaholism, Watson realised, was just inverse sprezzatura: making things look more difficult than they needed to be as a kind of false refuge.

The danger with ultra-professionalism is that it can be misinterpreted as always being busy, or at least always looking busy. This degenerates into the art of professional self-frazzling: instead of getting stuff done while keeping things in proportion, this is the tactic of looking visibly overwhelmed so that no one asks you to do any actual work. Having fun starts to look risky, which creates much bigger vulnerabilities.

I learnt the hard way. My worst season as a player was the most narrowly focused (I basically gave up everything except batting). And my best two seasons coincided with taking on off-field challenges (exams at university, and then, six years later, writing a diary of the 2003 season that was published as *On and Off the Field*, 2004). Professionally, my experience was unexceptional. In a study of elite scientists, Robert Root-Bernstein (himself awarded the MacArthur Fellowship, or 'genius grant') found that the highest-achieving academics believed that having hobbies added value to 'their scientific efficiency and thus to their careers'. (Lower achievers thought hobbies were 'irrelevant'.)

Second, can the *thing itself* retain the spirit of a game? Alexander Fleming was described disapprovingly as treating research like a game – 'I play with microbes … it is very pleasant to break the rules and to be able to find something that nobody had thought of' – but it led him to discover penicillin. What's true for research is true for making decisions. If you don't find a way to have fun while making decisions and leave openness intrinsic to the process, you're unlikely to be very good at them. Anyone can allow themselves to get ground down; real play is hard.

The best players finish practice when they are in full flow. 'The best way is always to stop when you are going good,' Hemingway said of writing, 'and when you don't know what will happen next.'

In my early thirties, I was slightly baffled to be invited by the CEO of a famous consultancy to offer my strategic advice. Having none, I fell back on a simple observation: of all the employees I walked past on the way to his office door, he looked the least jaded and exhausted. A credit to him? Or an indictment of the working culture he presided over?

The relationship between low-level grind and concentrated play is like the difference between imprisonment on a running machine and playing an expressive rally in tennis. 'We don't stop playing because we grow old,' quipped George Bernard Shaw, 'we grow old because we stop playing.' It turns out Shaw's adage wasn't just a good line. Amateur tennis players enjoy an extra seven years of life expectancy; joggers drop dead right on time with everyone else.

Without play and lightness, any process is vulnerable – to depletion, to exhaustion, to collapse. Things might hold for a while, even allow a period of success; but it's extremely hard to sustain.

Play replenishes itself. Roger Federer gave us a perceptive hint here when he said 'I need change, I need a different point every time.' Millions of shots – *almost* exactly the same as countless times before – but never *the same point twice*, meaning an experience entirely boxed off and closed, without any scope for imagination or fun.

Simple play

On 27 November 2014, cricket went into shock after the sudden death – while batting – of the Australian opening batter Phillip Hughes.

Matches were abandoned or suspended, including the second day of New Zealand's Test match against Pakistan. Both sides debated whether the game should continue, especially considering the deep friendships with Hughes on the New Zealand side that went back to Under-19 days.

In the end, the match was played out to a conclusion, but

in a unique atmosphere. The sledging and backchat vanished instantly. The two teams just played cricket, no words needed.

The captain, Brendon McCullum, viewed that traumatic week as a turning point for his New Zealand side:

> What we saw was a group of guys who really banded together and tried to help one another out and I guess just focus on getting people through the game rather than worry about the result ...
>
> Bizarrely, the way we went about playing with I guess less care of the result or the outcome led us to probably one of our most famous Test wins overseas [McCullum made 202], and from that moment there've been elements that we've tried to capture.
>
> And try to understand that there's a game that we play, and that it's not life or death ... So go out there and try to have a good time, don't worry if you get out and try and enjoy just being around a group of mates representing your country on the international stage.

McCullum struck a deep insight when he said that he wanted to 'strip it all back' to essentials. Instead of over-engineered thinking and management waffle, McCullum wanted a small number of people to take ownership for how the team played cricket – staying close to self-expression and, above all, play.

Though open to innovative ways of doing things, McCullum took the view that where things could be simpler, they should be simpler. And without *unnecessary complexity*, fragility wouldn't slip into the system. A few good people would set the agenda and keep things on track.

Since that day in UAE in 2014, as well as contesting three World Cup finals in white-ball cricket, New Zealand have played 59 Tests, winning 32, losing 18 and drawing 9. Over the previous 59 Tests, New Zealand had won 12, lost 27 and drew 20. They remembered how to play. And play has proved hard to beat.

12
Names for Things

Because I started playing cricket professionally when I was at university, the tag stuck that I was academic. Half-true. Different types of learning were always jumbled up for me.

In fact, university was better for my voice as a cricketer – perhaps by giving me a sense of proportion – than for my voice as a writer. Having learnt to succeed at exams, I had to *unlearn* that voice in my twenties when I started writing books. And unlearning is much harder than learning.

Ironically, it was studying as a history undergraduate that led me to this salutary paragraph by the philosopher Bryan Magee:

> It is a characteristic defect of the academic type of person that he tries to live his life and relate to reality, including other people, much too much in terms of concepts – by contrast to the man in the street, or the administrator, or the man of action, or the artistic type of person, all of whom live more in terms of ... direct experience.

That is exactly why I'm so glad I've worked in professional sport: it allowed me to relate my ideas to experience, not just to theory – not to live 'too much in terms of concepts'.

My 'career' (if that's the right term) in my twenties was full of contradictions and surprises. Academia initially prevented me from taking cricket too seriously – a sense of proportion which I promptly lost (temporarily) as a full-time professional. But playing sport was giving the writer in me something very different: the experience of winning and losing, and making sense of those experiences directly. Ironically, academic study was useful for my cricket, and cricket anchored my thinking in the real world.

But I never quite left academia, and stayed in liminal spaces between theory and practice. For five winters, aged 20 to 25, I lived in an East Village New York apartment belonging to a professor of philosophy and joined an entirely non-cricketing scene. That circle – conversation, music, ballet, opera – was esoteric but unpretentious, bringing together performance, academia and bohemia. The setting of St Marks Place, with its quirky bars and tattoo parlours, was gloriously remote from the Oxbridge world where many people seemed imprisoned by the same social set, 'progressing' almost involuntarily from 'a good school' to 'a good university' into 'a good London job' before finally, I guess, 'a good golf club'.

The ultimate currency in that St Marks Place circle was creative achievement. Bringing a creative vision to life – *any* creative vision – transcended academic learning or cleverness (even if those skills sometimes helped at the margins). Cleverness was incidental; there were more important things. You can win arguments while still losing at life – and vice versa. New York's East Village, more than three years at Cambridge, was my real university.

Names for things

How useful did I find 'formal' learning at the sharp end of sport?

Richard Feynman distinguished between 'knowing things and knowing the names for things'. But having 'names for things' – drawn from academic study and research – can help you identify them earlier and more clearly, even at the sharp end of practical experience.

Selectors, of course, are routinely accused of persevering with players for too long, out of stubbornness or flat-out denial. An occasional refresher on the economics concept of **sunk capital** is a sobering reminder that having wasted a lot of money already shouldn't persuade you to waste even more.

In 2011, I met up with Daniel Kahneman. He had famously identified, while observing the training of Israeli pilots in the 1960s, how the mathematical concept of **regression to the mean** had implications in the very human sphere of teaching and learning. The instructors were overestimating the effect of their feedback on the trainee pilots: performance was simply regressing to the mean.

Regression to the mean continues to wrong-foot decision-makers in sport (as data analysts can attest from listening to coaches talk about players' historical performances). Consider a player with a decent but not stellar track record in a large sample of domestic T20s matches. In a much smaller sample of international matches, he has a far better average. One of three things could be happening. Either international cricket has mysteriously become easier than domestic cricket (not true); or the player is more adept on the bigger stage (possible but not likely); or, in a matter of time, his international performances will level off and find the level of his general aptitude (very likely) – otherwise known as regression to the mean. Coaches and selectors can spend a lot of time interrogating reasons for things where no reasons exist: the relevant facts just aren't in yet.

There were many times in cricket selection that Kahneman's frameworks provided useful warnings. 'We tend to have a hero or an actor operating in a situation,' Kahneman observed, 'wherever possible we'll keep the situation fixed and have the actor move.' But of course it's often the hero who's unchanged and the situation that has moved on. This is the **focus rule**. It warns you about being tricked into thinking that a manager or captain has suddenly become brilliant when in fact he's making the same quality of decisions, but two superb players have returned to fitness and are making him look good.

Misled into overestimating a player because he reminds you of someone else who was a superstar? That's the **representativeness bias**. When people say in selection meetings, 'He reminds me of …', it's likely they are short of evidence and looking to beef up their advocacy.

Because one good batting innings can last all day, cricket is especially vulnerable to **recency bias**. One striking performance *yesterday* shouldn't be allowed to overturn a fair ranking of two players made over a large sample size.

I owe to Chris Dillow, author of the blog *Stumbling and Mumbling*, my understanding of **revenge effects**, another concept from economics. Dillow wrote that one of my articles on cricket – exploring how over-professionalism could become a straitjacket against self-expression – was a case study in revenge effects, only without using the term (I didn't know it).

Ever since, I've been alert to revenge effects. The entire history of batting technique, of course, is one revenge effect after another. You are nicking too many balls to the slips, so you guard against vulnerability on the outside edge by moving across to the off-side. Which means you get LBW too much – even more than you were getting out caught in the slips. Many technical 'tweaks' end up with far more serious consequences than the coach (or player) expected. Any idea, however sensible it sounds, can not only be taken too far, it can entirely swamp the whole enterprise.

Sport can learn just as much from historical theory, especially thinking about **indeterminacy**. The assumption that what did happen *was always going to happen and only could have happened* is the foundational error that wrong-foots much analysis of sport. It can be a painful exercise, but I tried to look for the influence of chance when things went well rather than just when things went badly. In Sri Lanka in 2018–19, the Test team won a sparkling series 3–0. We also won all three tosses, and gained the advantage of batting first each time. Examining luck, instead of harnessing it as an excuse, is more useful in tempering overconfidence. Since researching and writing *Luck* (2012), and now having had spells back at the sharp end inside sport, I realise how thinking about randomness and indeterminacy shaped and informed my thinking about sport as a practitioner.

It is especially difficult to escape being fooled by randomness in sport, perhaps more than in other spheres. On the one hand, sport is extremely effective at building randomness into the drama (a lucky goal, a mistaken refereeing decision, the bounce of the ball). And yet, having opened up opportunities for chance, sport then cuts the other way. One of the ways in which sport seduces us is by satisfying our desire for clarity. Sport yields a result, which serves as a kind of resolution.

The literary critic Steven Connor includes a superb section on this theme in his book *A Philosophy of Sport* (2011). First, sport creates the conditions in which skill and chance can and must interact:

> Sports and games are a dramatization of what John-Paul Sartre has called the necessity of our contingency ... In it [sport], the necessary and the contingent are so tightly, and paradoxically, bound together ... Sport is an actualization of chance ... a kind of counting out or working through of chances.

Yct sport's protagonists, having volunteered to jump into a context in which they are surrounded by chance, are simultaneously seeking to *overcome* their exposure to luck by asserting their superior skill and willpower. This is what the greatest players find irresistible about sport: they are addicted to the feeling of trying to force order and control over indeterminate surroundings:

> There are two contrasting intentions in this. One seeks to overcome chance, imposing purpose and direction upon the indefinite; but the other overcomes chance only by subjecting oneself to it, playing with it and against it – playing it out ...

This is the paradox of sport. It 'multiplies indeterminacy', before converting indeterminacy into a single and brutal conclusion. One answer – the score – emerges from many possibilities. That prompts Connor's conclusion (which explains how hard it can be to make sense of sport):

> The aim of sport is to raise (unless one had better say reduce) the potential to the actual ... The sporting event aims to *force evidence into manifestness.* [My italics.]

I'd make some additions to Connor's insights. Yes, the *score* is aiming to force evidence into manifestness. But a decision-maker has got to be better than that.

The score is not the whole of reality, because the score doesn't perfectly reflect performance. And that's exactly how Brentford FC found an edge by using the metric of 'expected goals', and how England cricket benefited from using 'weighted averages'. The score is loosely correlated (we'll come back to that phrase) with the underlying performance. But they are not exactly the same thing.

Rasmus Ankersen, who adopted expected goals at Brentford before it was widely emulated elsewhere, has explored the tension between results and the league table (and the implied injustice contained in that tension):

> In football there is a frequently used expression: 'the league table never lies' ... Everyone gets what they deserve. It is not that simple actually. If you want to understand how a gambler thinks, there is one concept you have to get: the league table always lies ... Even 38 games – a full season – is a very small sample size, not enough to strip out randomness from the equation.

Football, it is true, is especially exposed to luck because the size of the scoring unit is so big. A lucky goal stays influential over the result in the way that a lucky 2-pointer in basketball is less likely to be.

But Ankersen's insights apply to all sports. As a consequence, first you need to create measuring systems which are *less* fooled by randomness (on-base percentage, expected goals, weighted averages). Second, understanding luck and indeterminacy must inform not only your data-systems but also your decision-making *disposition*.

The revealed 'answer' of any sports match, tournament or league superficially appears to prove that the winning approach was the *superior* approach all along. But of course that isn't true. As the poker player Annie Duke argues in *Thinking in Bets* (2018), success is only 'loosely correlated' with good decision-making. You can make the right decisions, as any poker player will tell you, and still lose the hand. And you can be wrong and win. Over the short term, that is.

The difficulty is living with that loose correlation, and the uncertainty of your own agency, while continuing to make the next set of decisions.

A first-rate decision-maker can say: 'I lost this hand, but that shouldn't knock me off my strategy.' (*Holding your nerve.*) But he or she can also say: 'I won, but I'm not sure I got the decisions right.' (*Avoiding hubris.*)

An effective decision-maker constantly walks that tightrope. Too much belief (sometimes in the face of the short-term evidence) risks resilience tripping over into the territory of overconfidence. Too much hastiness to throw everything overboard makes it impossible to learn anything because strategy is always in flux before sufficient evidence is in.

The job of a decision-maker is to disentangle skill, luck and circumstance – and that's incredibly hard.

Is a correlation between current strategy and performance becoming inarguable? What quantity of winning or losing represents a convincing pattern? There is no single answer to the question of how much evidence is required before it is conclusive. Again, it can only be a matter of judgement.

Sports humanities

I mostly stumbled on these models and frameworks through accidental discoveries and chance encounters in my thirties: a newspaper sent me to interview Nassim Taleb; a magazine set up a meeting with Daniel Kahneman; *Luck* took me to Stanford and a conversation about uncertainty with Kenneth Arrow.* All were pursued for no deeper reason than that they seemed interesting at the time. Only in retrospect did I discern that they'd all given me theoretical frameworks about sport and decision-making that I'd be able to turn to practical ends in my forties.

An intermediate step was creating a home, an 'academic' institution, for studying the interaction of theory and practice in sport.

Fifteen years ago, Middlesex County Cricket Club asked me to become their captain. What could I do to make myself a better leader and decision-maker? I'd already had university experiences in the UK and America and I was lucky to be connected in education. Was there a postgraduate course where

---

* While listening to dodgy predictions based on bogus stats inside sport, I remember Arrow's classic story from World War Two, when some Air Force officers were asked to provide weather forecasts for one month ahead. Arrow demonstrated that these 'forecasts' did not improve on randomness. When this was pointed out to the top brass, the reply was handed down: 'The Commanding General is well aware that the forecasts are no good. However, he needs them for planning purposes.'

contrarian thinkers across sport could exchange ideas? I couldn't find anywhere that was a good fit. That gap in the market stayed at the back of my mind.

A decade later, when I was teaching a History MA programme, I saw another problem. Sport was often isolated at the margins of university study, stuck in the silos and departmental separation within modern universities. There was sports science, there was sports marketing, there was sports psychology. But what about a wider interdisciplinary approach, helping leaders understand and apply frameworks and models from across the academic spectrum? First, as a professional sportsman and then, second, as an academic, I felt there was a gap in the way sport was addressed inside academia.

At the outset of creating something new, I encountered the classic objections to innovation: but where does this fit within the bureaucracy ... shouldn't it be more like something that already exists ... it would be so much easier if ... but an alternative ready-made home could be ...

Fortunately, the idea of creating something new and different was backed by the educationalist Sir Anthony Seldon (who was then Vice-Chancellor of the University of Buckingham) and the entrepreneur Andrew White – and together we founded the Institute of Sports Humanities (ISH) in 2018. We wanted ISH to be inherently practical and interdisciplinary – some history, some behavioural economics, some psychology, some sports business. Bringing together different strands of sport helps the cross-fertilisation of ideas. ISH's mission is to inspire sport's present and future leaders and, in the process, to encourage collaboration between academia and elite sport. Today, after three cohorts in London and educating leaders across many different sports, ISH is expanding in Australia and India.

I was writing the first course syllabus – the MA Leadership in Sport – at the time when England approached me about the selection role. And I continued to teach the decision-making module when I was professionally busy with the practical challenge of selection with England. Just as the combination of studying and playing had been good for my cricket in my own student days, teaching decision-making now proved a counterpoint and stimulus for challenges I faced as a selector.

This was helped by the MA students' talent for focusing on prescient case studies. One dissertation explored the counter-intuitive recruitment strategy of the LA Rams (they always trade a 1st-round draft pick on the principle that 1st-round picks are over-valued), just as the Rams began their march towards winning the NFL in 2022. Another focused on how Brentford FC pioneered the metric of expected goals to measure performance (beyond the headline scoreboard), a similar approach to England cricket's weighted averages. A third student made a statistical study of the most efficient time to make substitutions in Premier League football, revealing how fan and media pressure affects managerial decisions.

Work with England helped me to explain models and approaches we explored at the Institute. Work at the Institute provided new and different examples and analogies for my work with England.

Founding and then growing ISH with Andrew White was a new experience of complementary approaches and differing kinds of intelligence. Andrew is an entrepreneur; I'm not. In our day-to-day conversations, I saw how Andrew – given a glimpse of the chess board – could internalise not only the positions of all the pieces, but also the likely upcoming moves and patterns of play. After the fact, I was sometimes able to describe quite well and clearly a plan or an insight that Andrew had reached, in the classic tradition of entrepreneurial imagination, instantly and intuitively.

There's a perceptive story told by the Argentinian footballer and thinker Jorge Valdano, who had first-hand experience of Diego Maradona's second, wondrous goal against England in the 1986 World Cup. 'I am certain I can describe it much better than he could,' Valdano reflected. 'But I could never have scored it.' Valdano later added:

> With that sentence I only wanted to establish the difference between narrative intelligence and footballing intelligence. The first has more prestige but the second has more complexity ... Great football to me is the art to improvise, to find solutions.

At times in my business conversations with Andrew, substituting the word 'football' for the word 'business', I feel like Valdano observing Maradona – nearby, but several steps behind (however clear-sighted in retrospect).

Andrew got there early on the cricket, too. 'You have to understand', he said to me on my first day as selector, 'that they are going to sack you. Because you are going to do things. All the more reason to crack on and not waste a day.' Good advice.

Self-reliance

This chapter sets up a contrast between theory and practice. But at a certain level, perhaps intellectual and practical pursuits are reunited. To achieve anything heroic, both the thinker and the practitioner must do what they believe is right, resting on independent confidence that is individual and intuitive.

Despite my scepticism and awareness of the dangers of overconfidence, I can't deny that the most important factor in the way I make decisions is trust in my own instincts and the willingness to go my own way.

I recently stumbled on Ralph Waldo Emerson's famous essay *Self-Reliance* (1841). Both the disinterested intellectual and the practical man of affairs, Emerson argues, must follow their own intuitive lodestar, no matter how much criticism it attracts:

> What I must do is all that concerns me, not what the people think. This rule, equally arduous in actual and in intellectual life, may serve for the whole distinction between greatness and meanness ... The great man is he who in the midst of the crowd keeps with perfect sweetness the independence of solitude.

Emerson contrasts the dangerous conformity of 'Society' (which 'loves not realities and creators, but names and customs') with 'self-trust' ('a man should learn to detect and watch that gleam of light which flashes across his mind from within'):

> Society is a joint-stock company, in which the members agree, for the better securing of his bread to each shareholder, to surrender the liberty and culture of the eater.

Be wary about any intellectual cowardice you might accept, Emerson concludes, in order to 'get on' in any career. Nonconformity is what gives a life greatness. (Emerson's essay was an inspiration to Edward Hopper, whose 'Notes on Painting' (1933) quoted Emerson's aphorism: 'Speak your latent conviction, and it shall be the universal sense.')

What Emerson and Hopper admire in the artist is exactly the quality Howard Marks observes in all good investors: the ability to take 'uncomfortably idiosyncratic positions'. This is, I think, perhaps the only thread that connects all different kinds of talents (whether business, artistic or intellectual): the confidence to act on what they believe, however difficult the implications. Originality, powered by independence, which in turn demands the acceptance of discomfort.

To be a good practical decision-maker, however much theoretical support is on hand, you will feel very alone – and yet also be inspired and emboldened by this exposed and peculiar form of loneliness. Taking a position becomes its own reward. Success, in the phrase of the great England cricketer Graham Gooch, is an 'inside job'.

But there's a second problem, which even bravery can't help with. How much 'self-trust' is too much? When *can't* your intuitions be relied on? There is no complete answer – beyond awareness that it is another judgement, another balance.

13
'Stand There'

In 2016, I was consultant to Royal Challengers Bangalore at that year's edition of the Indian Premier League. The team had attracted so many highly gifted players, especially batters. During practice sessions, in terms of studying great talent, it was hard to know where to start. Almost involuntarily, I found myself gravitating towards the net of A. B. de Villiers, and I think what drew me was the sound. De Villiers's movements were so pared down; and yet the strike of his bat was so clipped and clean – focus and calm before lethal finesse.

Perhaps that's why opponents and coaches, however gritty and down to earth, have often attributed to de Villiers a sixth sense about the next ball – bouncer, yorker, slower delivery, somehow he seemed to *know*. This, I suggest, is an illusion. Yes, the best batters, fractionally earlier and more accurately than their peers, do pick up and respond to tiny movements or 'tells' given away in the bowler's delivery stride. But this isn't really about second-guessing, let alone 'premonition'. We talk a lot about superior shot-selection, but what do we really mean by that? Is it that some players are almost clairvoyant, or is it (as I believe) that the best players, having more shots at their disposal – de Villiers's nickname is 'Mr 360' – *can wait for longer before making up their minds*? (Though obviously we are dealing in milliseconds.)

When I spoke with de Villiers, he downplayed specific prediction and instead stressed time and a sense of awareness: 'When I played rugby I could time a pass, find space, put a man through the gap. It's the same thing.'

It's tempting to invest great players with almost paranormal powers when you watch them respond to each problem with the perfect solution, but in fact what they are doing is waiting longer. The choices they make are superior because they take more time over them. No need to *predict* if you trust completely your capacity to *react*.

The endurance of trust ends in the creation of time. When I joined up with the New York Mets in 2001, I learnt the classic adage for baseball hitters: 'Wait-wait-wait; quick-quick-quick.' (The same logic explains why deceleration has become a key metric in basketball. When James Harden was flying high in 2016, Marcus Elliott of P3 Applied Sports Science explained what made him special: 'Harden is barely average in almost every metric we look at related to athleticism, except for his deceleration metrics ... In those he's one of the best we've ever measured in any sport.' Harden could slow down faster than anyone else, creating extra space for his shooting.)

The great players deceive us. They don't *have* time so much as *create* it. And the only way to 'create' time is to postpone the moment when you initiate the process of running out of it.

'Preliminary' squad

In the decision-making sequence ahead of the 2019 World Cup, there was one last curveball. The International Cricket Council (ICC), which runs all major international tournaments, demands that every team submits an early squad for planning and marketing purposes. In spring 2019, this 'preliminary squad' had to be announced on 17 April. Usually, this preliminary squad, barring illness or injury, is the same squad that boards a plane and heads off to the competition a few weeks later.

Except, as the host country in 2019, England weren't going to be boarding a plane. We were here already. And, crucially, the preliminary squad was exactly that: preliminary. There was one last opportunity to make changes five weeks later, when our final squad had to be named irrevocably on 23 May – a week ahead of the first match of the tournament.

Usually, most people would say: get your squad finalised as soon as possible. What's the benefit of distinguishing between the need to submit a preliminary squad and the final date a few weeks later, right on the eve of the tournament? Why wait and create extra uncertainty? Indeed, a perfectly rational case could have been made for an early and 'decisive call' (note the moral approval) on the issue. Further, England's circumstances included, of course, the late qualification of Jofra Archer. He had qualified for England by 17 April and was eligible for selection. Given all the points made in the earlier chapter, and considering just how good he is, why delay adding him to the World Cup squad?

That wasn't the decision we made. We kept the preliminary squad of 17 April in line with the group that had recently toured the West Indies in February–March. But we simultaneously added Archer to the playing group – an enlarged squad of 17 – that would play the warm-up matches before the World Cup itself.

This had several advantages, as head coach Trevor Bayliss shrewdly argued. It gave Jofra the opportunity to earn his final World Cup place in a way that everyone could follow and understand. Everyone had seen how good he was for Sussex and the Rajasthan Royals. But that was not the same as seeing it in an England shirt.

Naming 17 players for the warm-up matches also created an opportunity for a last look at all the tactical permutations, which could be – and indeed were – influenced right up to the wire by fitness concerns and the resulting squad balance between bat and ball.

So we announced two squads for the same format simultaneously (the only time we ever did this). The first was a 17-man squad to play against Ireland and Pakistan in the warm-up matches (with Archer). The second was a 15-man preliminary World Cup squad (no Archer). I tried to make this second announcement in such a way that it sounded very ... provisional. We wanted to give the impression that we knew Jofra was an exceptional player, and there was scope and time for talent to rise to the top. But we also wanted it to emerge organically, with a sense of justice and fairness to others – as well as to him.

In summary: a preliminary squad was announced (with inbuilt hints of last-minute changes), with a second squad announced simultaneously (even though we were only weeks away from a massive tournament).

This context left me, as head of selection, with a slightly bizarre press conference to deliver on 17 April. The drum-roll for the World Cup selection was gathering volume, and we were honour-bound to reveal the preliminary squad. But we were also bringing Jofra into the fold for the first time. So at first glance, the two big stories of the day – here's Jofra ... and now here's the preliminary squad – pointed in different directions.

The reader will have spotted that this sequence of decisions was vulnerable to criticism. It wouldn't take much to spin them as 'last-minute' or 'over-engineered' or 'creating stress at a demanding moment in team life'. (That narrative was there, ready to be rolled out, if one of two things had happened: first, if Jofra hadn't succeeded. Second, if England hadn't succeeded.)

But at the time of those decisions on 17 April, the underlying risks did not increase by leaving the squad unchanged for the preliminary squad (without Jofra). England lost nothing by using the full allocation of time at our disposal. It would have been easy, with such a big decision occupying all our minds, to seek 'clarity' and show 'decisiveness'. Easy and mistaken.

The business writer Jim Collins has argued that the difficulty of continuing to leave open a difficult choice can lead decision-makers to rush the decision itself:

> People have such a need to resolve ambiguity and uncertainty that they often act quicker than they need to because it's dealing with their own need to make the uncertainty go away ...
>
> But the uncertainty *never* goes away.

There is a pithier version among doctors: 'Don't just do something. Stand there!'

In the case of the 2019 World Cup, the extra time allowed room for events to unfold, events that suited England. Within a couple of matches of watching Jofra bowl, England fans and colleagues alike could see he was special. Andrew Flintoff, the heroic ex-England all-rounder, had a typically quotable one-liner about Jofra. When Flintoff was pressed about which player could possibly make way for Archer, given the strength and unity of the team that had already reached number one, Flintoff paused for effect before concluding it had to be ... 'Anyone!'

Flintoff went on to say, fast bowler about fast bowler, 'I was watching him the other day and I just found it so frustrating that a bloke can bowl so fast with what looks like so little effort ... He's got to be in.' Flintoff's sentiment captured the wider mood of England cricket fans. Everyone could see it now. Which is exactly what Trevor Bayliss and Eoin Morgan had hoped would happen.

Messages after 10 p.m.

Plenty of decision-making experiences could be used to advance exactly the opposite case: that some decisions are best made quickly.

One evening I got back to my hotel room after dinner and saw a string of messages on my phone. A rule of thumb when you are part of management in a sports team – lots of messages after 10 p.m. mean one thing: a problem. A player had been suddenly ruled out of tomorrow's match and an impromptu conversation about communication and selection was needed in the head coach's room.

By the time we gathered – captain, coach, selector – it was closer to 11 p.m., and I began by laying out what I thought were the options, describing them as neutrally as possible. The funny thing about last-minute 'crises' in sports teams is that they often don't feel stressful. Minds focus, but with a lightness and a sense of mischief. Here we all are, apparent grown-ups, but talking late into the night about a match that's due to start in a matter of hours. There isn't space for grandstanding or process, just shorthand and fun.

Joe Root listened carefully before very clearly articulating his preference. His logic was sound and robust – we'd all said we wanted a balanced attack, and we were going to stick with that principle. Decision made? Yes, decision made. Everyone agreed.

Here's the thing. In this instance, we had nearly 12 hours left to run down the clock before the decision had to be made. Why not use the last 12 hours?

Because in this case the underlying risks *were* changing. The decision might occupy everyone's mind overnight, when rest and clarity were called for. No new information was likely to come to light before the toss at 10.30 the next day. The options were already obvious and completely known. Delaying the decision was likely only to add stress to already busy minds.

After a complex day, the final decision had emerged with pleasing clarity and speed. And the atmosphere was happy and relaxed as we split up towards our various corners of the team hotel.

I had one last stat for Joe as we stood at the door. 'You know we have a 100 per cent winning record when there is ... a selection meeting after 10.30 at night due to circumstances out of our control.' That summed up the mood in the room. It's fun making decisions under pressure, including time pressure. And the 100 per cent winning sequence held for that match, too.

Time and risk

Without delay ... hasty ... over-eager ... impetuous ...
Considered ... indecisive ... bogged down ... ponderous ...

Both these sets of associated words constitute a spectrum of descriptive terms applied to decisions. And moral judgements, clearly, are built into each of them.

When it suits us, we might describe our own decisions as considered (if we want to emphasise due process) or, in a different set of circumstances, that the decision was made *without delay* (look how decisive I am).

But if we are sitting in judgement (and unimpressed) by someone else's decision, how easy it is to put a pejorative slant on things. If the decision is made quickly, and we don't like it, we say it's hasty. If the decision is made slowly, and we don't like it, it's ponderous or over-thought.

The amount of time taken to make a decision – or, more accurately, the amount of time the decision is assumed to have taken – is confidently inserted into the narrative. Rushed. Sclerotic. Decisive. Carefully weighed. We often learn as much about the onlooker in these remarks as we do about the decision itself.

So what *is* the right amount of time to take over an important decision? More specifically, is there any correlation between speed of decision-making and quality of outcome? Jim Collins set out to answer both these questions in his book *Great by Choice* (2011). The answer, he found, depended entirely on the nature of the risk under consideration. There is, in other words, nothing intrinsically good about making a decision quickly or making it slowly. The key question isn't the time it takes to decide. It's whether the risk level is changing as time ticks by:

> The '10X' leaders [the leaders of highest-performing companies] had a much wider range of ability between slow, medium and fast [decisions]. And sometimes they made really big decisions quickly. And sometimes they made really big decisions slowly. And there didn't seem to be a pattern.

Collins reflected that we are duped into lumping all decisions into the same kind of process and a similar time frame. Instead:

> The question is not 'Fast decision or slow decision' as proxies for 'Decisive or not?'
>
> It's: 'How much time before your risk changes?' And then make your decision within that time frame.

Time, in other words, is always the first question in decision-making. But the right question is not 'How much time should we take over this decision?' but instead, 'How much time do we have before it becomes a different kind of decision?'

When the risk changes, so does the urgency. But not before. That's why judgement about priorities and sequencing is so fundamental. The most important thing in work (and life) is figuring out which decisions need to be made, and how much time you have to make them.

'In form'

Even if the poise and calm of A. B. de Villiers is far out of reach, every professional batter has phases of form when the game feels deliciously simple:

> In tune with the tempo of the match.
> Alert to risks but not hyper.
> The ball clearer in vision and slower through the air.
> A split second longer to decide, a moment of grace to find a gap in the field.
> The ball arriving in rhythm with the swing of your bat.
> You have time to *decide* and, more often than not, it's the right decision.

Having time is exactly how we remember the *feeling of confidence*. What's true of decision-making in batting applies to decisions in life:

> Confident but not overconfident.
> Informed while also wary.
> Conscious of uncertainty but not daunted by it.
> Alert to risks changing over time, but unrushed and capable of living with decisions left open.
> Understanding consequences while still having fun.

Sometimes it takes a long time to realise the point of a story. When I was a young batter, the New Zealand player and coach John Wright told me, 'Ed, you really learn about batting when you've already scored a hundred.' I was a bit baffled at the time.

Everyone plays well when they've already scored a hundred. What I wanted to learn was how to get to a hundred more often. John was introducing the question of handling anxiety. All batters live with subliminal anxiety – about getting out, about failure, about being dropped. And when you've scored a hundred all those anxieties go away. And it's so much easier and clearer. Which was John's point. Can you learn to overcome anxiety before you've succeeded? Or, better put, reach an accommodation with anxiety – because then, paradoxically, you'll be far more likely to succeed.

This is connected with the art of negotiation. The game theorist John Nash demonstrated that protagonists bargain more effectively when they are less needy. The less you fear *not* getting what you want, the more likely you are to get what you want. The logical conclusion follows: in any negotiation, your best strategy is an internal as well as external question. Can you 'will' yourself into a state of relative indifference, and thereby negate anxiety-induced neediness?

The same point relates to decisions more generally. Even when the stakes are high – especially when the stakes are high – can you see through the fog of noise, get past neediness and anxiety, and attend simply to those things that need to be decided, in the right order, giving each decision the appropriate amount of time?

It is not about plugging into a system imported from elsewhere, or becoming like someone else, still less about trying to become a machine. We've got machines for that. Stay close to the bits that only humans can do.

And that rests on these very human requirements: the space to reflect, the curiosity to inspire analogy and surprise, the freedom to make mistakes and test ideas that don't work, the cunning and playfulness to get alongside your most productive patterns of thought, independence so your decisions are really your own, the authority to give you the agency to bring decisions to life, and, above all, the time to live in your own head. In doing so, you are implicitly making another set of decisions: deciding how you want to live.

Under pressure and swamped by modern information overload, the default position for leaders and organisations – like the out-of-form batter – is to fill time. Instead, we need to reclaim it.

Long-term

A connected point, about trust and time, relates to long-term reputation.

After my first press conference in early summer 2018, an ECB communications official sent me a set of 'feedback' charts. They contained various metrics about how the 1st Test selection and its media communication had been 'received'. The feedback demonstrated that one article in one newspaper had been 'positive' about the selection. Another article in a rival media house had been 'negative'. A third article had been 'neutral' about the latest squad selection. And so on. Across the whole cricket media landscape, article after article was assessed and measured according to 'positiveness'.

Perhaps an algorithm was busy counting adverbs and adjectives in every written article? 'Bold' – one point; 'disappointing' – minus a point; 'confusing' – getting behind now; 'forward-thinking' – ah, back on an even keel.

But what if many of those adjectives and adverbs, all notching up towards an overall 'score', related to peripheral information?

Could the algorithm handle that? I wondered how this hypothetical sentence would have been scored: 'On a joyously sunny and gloriously optimistic early summer morning, with Lord's set fair for a brilliant summer of thrilling cricket ahead, the England selector announced a bad team.'

At first glance, the post-selection 'media feedback' looked very professional and 'objective', with charts and percentages giving the whole thing a 'scientific' feel. One final aggregate figure was designed to capture how well the selection had gone overall, with the various article 'scores' averaged out in a grand finale.

Besides not allowing unnecessary vanity into your life, there were deeper reasons for not poring over statistical analysis of how 'positively' selections were received: the habit of following the path of least resistance was a certain road to defeat. My job was to serve the team's needs, not to seek a good press.

Analogies between sport and politics are always inexact. But examples from politics can be instructive about how chasing the short term can damage long-term reputation. In April 2017, Theresa May led in opinion polls by about 20 per cent. May's lead proved so irresistible that she called a snap general election. It was a catastrophe. May lost her majority in the House of Commons, and soon after election day had a 'favourability rating' of minus 34 per cent. How did May's position collapse, in a matter of weeks, from (apparently) unbeatable to irreparable?

Paradoxically, May's PR team had done *too* good a job of inflating her reputation beyond the point at which it could be sustained. May's initial popularity *added* reputational fragility. Peak 'Mayism' had relied on convenient spin. After the turbulence of the Brexit referendum, May had been artfully positioned as a reassuring presence, the perfect captain of the ship in choppy political seas: no more pandering to the 24-hour news cycle; no running commentary on Brexit; substance and competence over style; steely rather than superficial and easy-going; long pauses suggesting deep thought. May's spin doctors turned her longueurs into moral and political qualities. That May didn't chase headlines became the new headline.

During the election campaign, every thread unravelled. There wasn't a running commentary on Brexit because there wasn't progress on which to comment. Brexit might mean Brexit – but what did that mean? There might not be a shallow 24-hour political agenda, but was there any agenda at all? The absence of style doesn't guarantee the presence of substance. A clearer reality emerged: a void had entered a vacuum and been cleverly presented as a virtue. When her reputational slide began, instead of slipping by a foothold or two, May careered all the way to the bottom of the mountain. Voters – real people, not communications professionals – felt duped. And the realisation of being duped led to a kind of revenge against the edifice of the mis-selling – May herself.

Even objectively great achievers can make a different version of the same mistake. Tiger Woods is one of the most successful golfers of all time. But at the height of Woods's career, his PR team weren't content with selling the image of a superb golfer to sponsors and corporates. They wanted something more universal. So a gloss about Woods's family values and down-to-earth unflashiness – the reliable father who drove a family saloon despite untold millions – was slathered on top of a genuine story of mastery. When Woods's private flaws were exposed, they became bound up with a wider reputational collapse. Had his pre-fall spin been less fraudulent, Woods would have received a more charitable assessment of his personal decisions. But after

Woods had been turned into a brand – a self-denying man-god – the public were less inclined to separate the golfer from the husband. Having projected the aura of a man totally intolerant of weakness, Woods became the victim of a backlash against his own cult of virtuous self-determination.

'All reviews ...'

There are three interconnected problems with chasing short-term 'communications wins'. To a certain type of decision-maker, the daily judgement of the media feels more pressing, more exciting and more important than other aspects of leadership, especially where success and failure are hidden from public view. Like addicts on social media, they become hitched to the dopamine hit of instant gratification. Hunting for 'good press' ends up exhausting their intellectual bandwidth.

Second, inflating reputation rather than earning reputation *increases* vulnerability to collapse – exactly what happened to Theresa May. Journalists don't like looking wrong in the final account. As reputation eventually settles towards the level of genuine achievement – as it always does in the end – the journalists who've assisted in inflating a reputation are forced into suddenly downgrading it.*

Finally, strategy should never be staffed out to media professionals so they can cast around for 'what might play well', holding their fingers up to the breeze. The public are remarkably savvy about being manipulated. Sniffing the influence of

* 'All reputation is hazardous, hard to win, and harder to keep' – William Hazlitt.

communications professionals, people just stop listening. Relying on 'comms' is now a very bad way to communicate.

There is no escape from the acid test: the verdict of time and long-term achievement. So you may as well ignore the headwinds (and tailwinds) of daily opinion.

'All reviews are bad for you,' reflected Ted Hughes, 'especially the good ones.' But we can add what the poet couldn't: understanding the longer game helped him to write poems that are read and admired decades later.

14 Back and Forward

In spring 2021, the ECB abolished the selection department. I left England cricket, and James Taylor's role changed from selector to chief scout. Full responsibility for selection was handed to the head coach, Chris Silverwood.

In making the decision, the ECB MD Ashley Giles argued that the new structure 'makes lines of accountability much clearer, with Chris Silverwood, as head coach, taking ultimate responsibility for picking England senior men's squads'.

On one level, we could all agree with that. Accountability (traditionally shared between captain, coach and selectors) did become clearer. But accountability cuts both ways. In difficult times, an emphasis on accountability can lead to a blame game. And cricket is a unique sport, with the captain given an unusual degree of decision-making autonomy on the field, and the existence of three different formats making selection a complicated puzzle.

The following year or so did prove difficult for England cricket. The Test team lost 8 games in the next 14, with one win and five draws. The final stages of managing high-performance sport through the Covid pandemic definitely made things harder for England. And untimely injuries, as ever, didn't help. The Test team had hoped to have its three fastest bowlers – Jofra Archer, Olly Stone and Mark Wood – fit and firing in Australia for the 2021–22 Ashes series. Sadly, Archer and Stone were unfit. At the T20 World Cup, England started superbly and looked like the team to beat, but narrowly lost a semi-final against New Zealand.

In early 2022, much of the cricket leadership changed, with MD Ashley Giles, head coach Chris Silverwood and assistant coach Graham Thorpe all moving on.

Andrew Strauss returned as interim MD (eventually followed by a full-time appointment, Rob Key). In announcing Chris Silverwood's departure, Strauss stated that the coach had been placed in 'an impossible situation' when the chief selector role had been added to his job as head coach. Chris was a close colleague of mine twice (first as a player at Middlesex, then when we were respectively selector and coach at England). He's a good man. I also felt the new structure and combined role was tough for him.

Having shrewdly appointed Brendon McCullum as head coach, one of Rob Key's first moves was to reinstate a selection panel, announcing he would begin a search for two full-time selectors (the system we had with James Taylor and me). 'The head selector role is one of the most important,' Key argued with characteristic directness, 'because you can have all this vision, all this philosophy, all the coaches, but if you have a selector who picks a bunch of numpties then you've got no chance have you really?'

In the future, I expect that England cricket will rejoin the wider trend across sport, and that Talent ID and selection will become more important than ever in shaping it.

There are also benefits in a structure that allows for some separation between selection and coaching. The independent positions James and I enjoyed as selectors reinforced our independent outlook. We both worked for England, without any county conflicts of interests. Independence from coaching gave us perspective and insulation from training-ground dynamics (the important thing is how good players are, not how amenable they are). We were also independent from the media. We challenged conventional thinking from the beginning and, as a result, faced scrutiny and pressure at the very outset – a good and healthy early test of our mettle.

Over the whole three years, we set out to think and act independently from external pressures, going through with decisions even when they were uncomfortable – perhaps especially when they were uncomfortable. Some quality of detachment was central to the task, and there was a danger that this would be interpreted as 'cold'.

When I finished as England selector, the broadcaster and former Hampshire captain Mark Nicholas wondered if I came across as 'aloof'. There are negative connotations within aloof: detachment to the point of a lack of warmth. And yet in some contexts the term could also be considered as having value, even virtue. Is it a bad thing for a judge, or the underwriter of large loans, to be considered aloof? We interpreted the new selection system as dispassionate, prepared to be unpopular when necessary, *independent*. So Nicholas's observation, in some respects, was close to the point of what we were trying to achieve. Better to be considered distant or hard to read than to be judged manipulated or fearful.

Perhaps this confidence came across to some as impertinent. In truth, it was very simple. We just wanted to win. And this unwavering aspiration – to win more – drove us to do what we believed in, even when it brought professional risk. True independence rests on freedom from anxiety about consequences.*

It is striking that we've lost much of the original meaning of the term *disinterested* (unbiased, free from obligations), as the word has drifted towards the previously distinct concept of *uninterested* (inattentive, indifferent). It is a mistake to confuse a detached manner – and approach – with being emotionally indifferent. I cared deeply about every match and every player. And I was fiercely competitive about England performing well: I felt responsible when we didn't.

How did I feel, then, about the role of chief selector suddenly being abolished and my exit from England cricket?

Sadness – definitely. Our group inside England cricket was close-knit and highly irreverent. We laughed a lot, often at ourselves. We have stayed close friends, but that collective jauntiness – towards each other and towards the outside world – no longer had the unifying purpose of the next decision, the next match.

Trust – not to 'manage' the situation. A strange thing to say when you are leaving, but I did have that trust. I made no attempt to influence public perceptions when I left England, and instead left cricket writers and the cricketing public to make

---

* C. S. Lewis's *Studies in Words* (1960) traces the development of the term 'free'. Free (legally); free (acting with justice) contrasted with bias and prejudice; free (of mind) rather than dependent on others. Lewis adds that this concept of freedom once existed through associations (now defunct) within the term 'liberal': thinking and acting with untrammelled independence rather than narrow career advancement.

their own assessments. I felt we had done well, and England's teams had flourished over a three-year period. Time would reach its own verdict, as it always does.

Space – in the weeks and months after leaving England, I made a very deliberate decision not to accept any invitations to broadcast or write about cricket, or to be interviewed in the media. I thought the best thing I could do for England cricket at that stage was to provide respectful space for the decision-makers at the sharp end.

Confidence – in our approaches and our ideas, because good ideas come through in the end; that's what makes them good. After an entire regime change, a year and a bit after I finished as selector, Rob Key (as new acting chief selector) and Brendon McCullum (as head coach) made a thrilling start to their period in charge. First, McCullum expressed interest in Adil Rashid, Jos Buttler and Moeen Ali returning to Test cricket – expanding the talent pool, and bringing multi-format stars back into contention. Second, McCullum double-downed on Jonny Bairstow as a specialist batter (Bairstow responded by blitzing four majestic hundreds in just three Tests). Third, under Ben Stokes's captaincy, England embraced a daring and counter-attacking style – which not only suited England's players but also engaged and uplifted the country. Pragmatism and principle in unison – powered by plenty of 'uninstitutional behaviour'.

And yet even now, in writing all this, a strange kind of self-criticism is close to the surface. Perhaps some readers may share it, too. Because there is a sense of detachment, even about a project I loved and a mission I believed in. Too much detachment? You may wonder and so do I.

Because once the chapter closed, I moved on. Teaching, thinking and writing once again took over. While I missed the jeopardy of high-performance sport, I enjoyed the freedom of having my time back and the absence of bureaucratic constraints. Something lost, something gained.

Hold on a minute. Can that be true? Can you switch, almost instantly, from total investment in trying to win cricket matches, to reflection and curiosity away from the pitch? Can anyone close the door like that and simply begin the next chapter? A mask of indifference – in the pursuit of fairness or sound judgement – is one thing. But what if the mask becomes the man? In other words, at what point do perspective and balance become a flaw? I don't know.

Another unresolved question: is an outsider's clear analysis a central part of what I bring to an organisation? Experience provides insights, but reflection informs strategy. To be most effective, I need alternate periods of time both inside and outside the practical sphere – without getting too settled in either domain. Put differently, every phase has its life cycle; and part of your usefulness is understanding the kind of qualities you can bring. I've never aspired to holding office, but to add value.

Perhaps my calm about leaving England cricket was bound up with something deeper. Because while my work as a selector had ended, the chapter was not closed. Yes, one side of my character – operating in the practical world of decisions and events – had played his hand and there was nothing more to be done. But the other side, the writer who makes sense of experience, had yet to do his job. And that was – that is – this book.

And in writing the book as I have, I feel doubly unguarded. It explores a set of decisions, rightly open to scrutiny and debate. More fundamentally, it reveals the interaction between my character and events as they happened – the person I am, to a significant degree.

In any business or organisation, it's always hard to disentangle people from structure, or know exactly how much each contributes to performance, because structure and people are always interacting. There is no structure so good that it can survive bad appointments. And sometimes flawed structures can be papered over by good people working effectively together.

Every structure or machine, as this book argues, relies on the human dimension. While we constantly tried to improve and refine our selection and Talent ID *systems* – from the scouting network to data analysis – above all, our collective output was defined by the interaction of complementary and independent approaches.

How should we approach a problem or decision? Nathan Leamon had a mathematician's tools. James Taylor brought the insight and craft of a recent England player. Mo Bobat saw how the whole organisation could inform as well as execute decisions. At the outset, Andrew Strauss had a strategist's sense of overall direction. The coaches and captains knew the feel of the dressing room and its dynamics.

All this brought together not only different opinions, but also differing kinds of knowledge – complementary to the system, and also complementary to each other. We respected each other's domain mastery as well as respecting each other as people. Our differences were our strengths – exactly the quality we hoped to create in the teams we were selecting.

The human–machine paradox

At times, England cricket has been accused of giving up too much authority to big data and algorithms.

In December 2020, Nathan Leamon used coded messages from the England dressing room to send signals to on-field captain Eoin Morgan during the T20 series against South Africa. England had checked that this was acceptable to the game's international governing body, the ICC, before the series began. The ICC confirmed the tactic did not breach any laws of the game. In fact, Leamon used the coded signals as visibly as possible, to avoid any subterfuge. In plain sight and using A4-sized characters, he placed one number and one letter in front of his laptop on the England balcony. The coded messages related to which bowler, according to the algorithm Leamon had built, Eoin Morgan should choose to deliver the following over.

Despite the transparency of the process and the confirmed legality of the tactic, the *Daily Telegraph* accused England of breaking the laws. 'Are England cheating?' wrote their chief cricket writer, Scyld Berry. 'That, in my opinion, is what they did in their last T20 international.' Michael Vaughan, who skilfully captained England in the epic 2005 Ashes series, argued that the system undermined the authority of the captain: 'If I were the England captain and the analyst suggested sending messages to me through signals from the dugout he would get short shrift.'

What was being underestimated here, I believe, is how the two parts of the system – cold data and human intuition – worked in tandem. Morgan was open to tactical steers from

Leamon's algorithm because he has deep confidence in his own judgement. He is very comfortable going his own way, potentially ignoring what the algorithm advises. Having extra information presented to him in the midst of battle didn't disorientate the captain, or make him double-guess himself. Some captains might prefer less information, in case it dominated their instincts or threw their judgement out of kilter. For Eoin, in contrast, the signals are simply another tool, one that he chooses to use – or not – as he sees fit. Once again, the usefulness of data, paradoxically, relies on the strength, not the weakness, of the human dimension.

As autumn follows summer

The advance and expanding influence of data is not a debate but a fact. Like gravity, it's inescapable. 'I hear people say we have to stop and debate globalisation,' Tony Blair said in 2005. 'You might as well debate whether autumn should follow summer.' The same point applies to data today.

In May 2022, Ukraine claimed to have killed 12 Russian generals on the front line during the opening months of the Russia–Ukraine war – a number that stunned military analysts. In tracking and locating key Russian targets, Ukraine was helped by American intelligence powered by data software companies.

Similar technologies had helped American intelligence to find Osama bin Laden. The hunt for bin Laden rested on a complex database and it was software engineers in Silicon Valley, rather than government agencies, who had the tools to find the signal in the data. 'A start-up called Palantir', Mark Bowden pointed out in *The Finish: The Killing of Osama bin Laden* (2012), 'came up with a program that elegantly accomplished what TIA [Terrorism Information Awareness program, set up in 2002] had set out to do.'

In June 2022, it was striking that the first executive from a Western country to be invited into Ukraine by President Volodymyr Zelensky was Alex Karp – CEO of Palantir Technologies. Zelensky stated he was 'delighted Palantir is ready to invest in Ukraine and help us in the fight against Russia on the digital front line'.

But a headline arguing that data software 'turned the war' in Ukraine would be at best incomplete. Without Zelensky's personal leadership – his bravery in rejecting the offer of evacuation; his turn of phrase ('I need ammunition, not a ride'); his determination to be present at street level in Kiev during the early days of the war; his emotional intelligence in representing his country's needs to other world powers; in short, conveying his own 'skin in the game' to his fellow citizens and the world – without all that, there would have been no war to be turned. Ukraine would have been routed in a matter of days.

Zelensky brought his people with him; data software supplied critical facts about the enemy. The president understood the power of appearances; data demonstrated the value of superior information. The one supported the other.

Predicting the rise of unpredictability

This book has mostly resisted prediction – until now.

Sport sets up a series of conflicts: attack versus defence, the collective versus the individual, expected strategy versus the unpredictable.

Increasingly, modern sports teams will use some version of AI to anticipate, plan for and respond to *what is most likely to happen next*. Self-learning algorithms use information about what has happened in the past to allocate probabilities about what may happen in the future.

This kind of information is especially useful in organising defensive systems. In a given pattern of play, if the percentage shot is likely to be a 3-pointer from the left of the court, it makes sense for the defence to load up its resources to make that play harder for the offensive team.

This trend, however, creates an opposite tension for the attacking team: if the defence is able to plan, with increasing precision, for what ought to happen, then the rational strategy is to do *what ought not to happen*. The unpredictable maverick returns once more, centre stage.

Sport's romantics may have the last laugh, after all. When a critical mass of players on the field is following a narrowly 'rational' strategy (which a computer could advise them to follow), the greater the advantage offered by the player who does what nobody could predict.

In other words, and in line with my confidence about talent and individualism, a new, higher kind of rationality emerges: every team will need unpredictability at its core.

In making decisions both on and off the field, though the human dimension can be augmented, it can never be replaced and it can never be eliminated.

Acknowledgements

I am extremely grateful to Ed Caesar, Jason Cowley, James Fox, Julian Glover, John Inverarity, Dan Jones, Mervyn King and Rebecca Smith for reading early drafts of this book and making very helpful and direct comments. Martin Trew applied his forensic eye, with incredible patience, to questions of style and clarity. All my books partly derive from conversations with my father – this one, too.

I was fortunate to work with many superb colleagues at England cricket. In my immediate team, James Taylor and Mo Bobat made the role of selector great fun as well as a great challenge. A selector is also only ever as good as the players available to select, so this book would be nothing without the cricketers who made England's teams so successful from 2018 to 2021.

The teachers, staff and students at the Institute of Sports Humanities consistently challenged and refreshed my thinking. Teaching is often a good way to learn.

My thanks to the editor of the *New Statesman* for permission to draw on two essays about Theresa May ('The Brexit Plague',

30 June 2017, and 'The Hollow PM', 13 October 2017) in Chapter 13 'Stand There', and also to the editor of the *Cricket Monthly* for permission to draw on my article on A. B. de Villiers ('Batting 3.0', July 2016) in the same chapter.

David Godwin read several drafts, making excellent suggestions, and always goes far beyond the role of 'agent' in his support. He also set up a great partnership with Arabella Pike and her brilliant team at William Collins. Arabella's insightful, speedy and practical advice transformed the book. The book also benefited from conversations with Howard Marks and Charlie Redmayne about leadership and decision-making.

Rebecca, Dexter and Margot Smith were patient during three years of long absences with cricket, and then gave me the space to write when I finally got back home.

Notes

Chapter 1 – Where Do 'We' Fit In?

Guy Griffith and Michael Oakeshott, *A Guide to the Classics: Or How to Pick the Derby Winner* (Revised edition. Imprint Academic, 2017).
Garry Kasparov. Interview with Elena Holodny, *Business Insider*, 24 May 2017, https://www.businessinsider.com/garry-kasparov-interview-2017-5?r=US&IR=T.

Chapter 2 – 'Uninstitutional Behaviour'

David Swensen – quoted in Howard Marks, 'Dare to be Great', Oaktree Memo, 7 September 2006, https://www.oaktreecapital.com/docs/default-source/memos/2006-09-07-dare-to-be-great.pdf?sfvrsn=2.
Howard Marks. Also in 'Dare to be Great', Oaktree Memo.

Chapter 3 – Swarm Harmoniser

Swarm Harmonisers. Jessica Flack and Cade Massey, 'All Stars', *Aeon*, 27 November 2017, https://aeon.co/essays/what-complexity-science-says-about-what-makes-a-winning-team.

Ed Smith, 'As Evidence Grows of Southpaw Supremacy, Have We Reached Peak Left-handedness?', *New Statesman*, 17 December 2017, https://www.newstatesman.com/politics/uk-politics/2017/12/evidence-grows-southpaw-supremacy-have-we-reached-peak-left-handedness.

Johan Cruyff – quoted in Simon Kuper, *Barça: The Inside Story of the World's Greatest Football Club* (Short, 2021).

Chapter 4 – The Shock of the New

Michael Lewis, *Moneyball: The Art of Winning an Unfair Game* (Revised edition, W. W. Norton & Company, 2004).

Nevada Smith – quoted in Zach Kram, 'The 3-Point Boom Is Far From Over', *The Ringer*, 27 February 2019, https://www.theringer.com/nba/2019/2/27/18240583/3-point-boom-nba-daryl-morey.

Caspar Berry – quoted in Nathan Leamon, *Hitting Against the Spin* (Constable, 2021).

Arnold Toynbee – quoted in Iain McGilchrist, *The Matter with Things* (Perspectiva Press, 2021).

Michael Cox, *Zonal Marking: The Making of Modern European Football* (HarperCollins, 2019), includes the quotes from Lizarazu, Aragonés, Xavi and Guardiola.

Matt Ridley, *How Innovation Works* (4th Estate, 2020), citing examples drawn from *Innovation and Its Enemies* (2016) by Calestous Juma.

Rasmus Ankersen. Conversation with the author.

Chapter 5 – Super Over

Simon Kuper, 'How to Pick a Winning Team', *Financial Times*, 12 September 2019.

Chapter 6 – 'Lego'

Daryl Morey – quoted in Michael Lewis, 'The No Stats All-Star', *New York Times*, 13 February 2009.

Juanma Lillo. Interview with Sid Lowe, 'The Brain in Spain', *The Blizzard*, Volume 1, June 2011.

Russell Ackoff, 'Systems Thinking Speech', 2 November 2015, YouTube, https://www.youtube.com/watch?v=EbLh7rZ3rhU.

Chapter 7 – Sources of Confidence

Carlo Ancelotti, *Quiet Leadership: Winning Hearts, Minds and Matches* (Penguin, 2017).

Mike Brearley, *The Art of Directing*, BBC Radio 4, March 2007.

Chapter 8 – Policy?

Alexander Chancellor – quoted in Charles Moore, 'The Spectator Notes', *Spectator*, 4 February 2017, https://www.spectator.co.uk/article/the-spectator-s-notes-2-february-2017.

Quentin Skinner, *Machiavelli* (Oxford University Press, 1981).

Chapter 9 – Process/Anti-Process

Howard Marks, 'Dare to be Great', Oaktree Memo, 7 September 2006.

Richard Feynman, *What Do You Care What Other People Think?* (W. W. Norton & Company, 2018).

Barton Biggs – quoted in Howard Marks, 'Dare to be Great'.

Irving Janis – quoted in Howard Marks, 'Dare to be Great'.

Chapter 10 – X-Ray Cricket

On height versus reach in basketball: Michael Lewis, *The Undoing Project – A Friendship that Changed the World* (Penguin, 2017).

Chapter 11 – Play On

Greg Chappell, 'Australia's Nasty Sledging Has No Place in the Game', *The Times*, 7 December 2021, https://www.thetimes.co.uk/article/greg-chappell-book-extract-australias-nasty-sledging-has-no-place-in-the-game-we-didnt-play-like-that-9ggq6dz8t.

Juanma Lillo. Interview with Sid Lowe, 'The Brain in Spain', *The Blizzard*, Volume 1, June 2011.

Niall Ferguson, 'Complexity and Collapse: Empires on the Edge of Chaos', *Foreign Affairs*, March/April 2010.

George Watson, 'The Decay of Idleness', *Wilson Quarterly*, Spring 1991.

Robert Root-Bernstein – quoted in Alex Soojung-Kim Pang, *Rest: Why You Get More Done When You Work Less* (Penguin, 2016).

Alexander Fleming – quoted in Patrick Bateson and Paul Martin, *Play, Playfulness, Creativity and Innovation* (Cambridge University Press, 2013).

Roger Federer. Interview with Calvin Tompkins, 'Anxiety on the Grass', *New Yorker*, 21 June 2010, https://www.newyorker.com/magazine/2010/06/28/anxiety-on-the-grass.

Brendon McCullum. Interview. 'From Brash to Beloved, McCullum to Bow Out in Style', 22 December 2015, https://www.cricket.com.au/news/feature/brendon-mccullum-international-retirement-feature-new-zealand-black-caps-australia-ramsey/2015-12-22.

Chapter 12 – Names for Things

Bryan Magee, *The Philosophy of Schopenhauer* (Clarendon Press, 1997).

Daniel Kahneman. Interview with the author. 'He Knew He Was Wrong', *Spectator*, 17 December 2011, https://www.spectator.co.uk/article/he-knew-he-was-wrong-daniel-kahneman-interview.

Chris Dillow, 'Revenge Effects', *Stumbling and Mumbling*, 24 January 2014, https://stumblingandmumbling.typepad.com/stumbling_and_mumbling/2014/01/revenge-effects.html.

Rasmus Ankersen, *TedX* talk, 2 April 2018, https://www.youtube.com/watch?v=Sy2vc9lW5r0.

Kenneth Arrow – quoted in Peter Bernstein, *Against the Gods: The Remarkable Story of Risk* (Wiley, 1998).

Jorge Valdano. Interview. 'Maradona, Mascherano and Philosophy', BBC, 4 November 2008, http://news.bbc.co.uk/sport1/hi/football/7690933.stm.

Chapter 13 – 'Stand There'

A. B. de Villiers. Interview with the author. 'Batting 3.0', *Cricket Monthly*, July 2016, https://www.thecricketmonthly.com/story/1027027/batting-3-0.

Marcus Elliott. Interview with Danny Chau. 'James Harden's Brilliance Is a Two-Way Mirror', *The Ringer*, 2 November 2016, https://www.theringer.com/2016/11/2/16037302/james-hardens-brilliance-is-a-two-way-mirror-b158d1bf2e22.

Jim Collins. Interview. 'Relationships v Transactions', *The Knowledge Project Podcast*, https://fs.blog/knowledge-project-podcast/jim-collins-2/.

Ed Smith, 'The Brexit Plague', *New Statesman*, 30 June 2017.